A YEN FOR YEN
CASHING BIG ON DREAMS...

A YEN FOR YEN
CASHING BIG ON DREAMS...

Deven Arora

LEADS PRESS
an imprint of
B. Jain Publishers (P) Ltd.
An ISO 9001 : 2000 Certified Company

A YEN FOR YEN
Cashing Big on Dreams...

Edition: 2006
Reprint Edition: July 2006

All rights are reserved. No part of this book may be reproduced, stored in a retrieval system or transmitted, in any form or by any means, mechanical, photocopying, recording or otherwise, without any prior written permission of the Author.

© Copyright with the Author

Price: Rs. 150. 00

Published by Kuldeep Jain for

LEADS PRESS
an imprint of **B. Jain Publishers (P) Ltd.**
1921, Street No. 10, Chuna Mandi,
Paharganj, New Delhi 110 055 (INDIA)
Phones: 91-11-2358 0800, 2358 1100, 2358 1300, 2358 3100
Fax: 91-11-2358 0471; *Email:* bjain@vsnl.com
Website: **www.bjainbooks.com**

Printed in India by
J.J. Offset Printers
522, FIE, Patpar Ganj, Delhi - 110 092
Phones: 91-11-2216 9633, 2215 6128

ISBN : 81-8056-642-0
BOOK CODE : BA-5882

Dedicated . . .

to my

loving parents

FOREWORD

Here you have everything — the ambition and arrogance of youth. The audacity of following dreams, however impossible and distant they seem. You have a story that spans continents and cultures, often with hilarious effect. Could any two cultures or places be more different? A garrulous Indian charmer and a taciturn Japanese sceptic?

Most of all you have the chance to see inside the heart as well as the mind of an extraordinary man and his extraordinary story.

In one sense, it is a story that belongs to its culture and its time – the language, the images, even the style of language is that of an Indian youth in the middle of the 20th century. But it has a larger relevance and a timeless one. It is about persistence and persuasion, sheer dogged determination and a real ability to meet people and to use them graciously but relentlessly to achieve objectives, a story relevant to our own times.

I have the pleasure and the honour to know Deven — he is every bit as remarkable as his story and he is true to life as his words. Enjoy.

Warmest
Stuart Walkley

Executive Vice-President, EMEA
Right Management Consultants
London SW1Y 4PE, UK

"Try not to become a man of success. Rather become a man of value."

Albert Einstein

PREFACE

I am Deven Arora. My life began in India during World War II, just before India's Independence. A college dropout, I moved to Japan at the age of 27 after having spent four years writing more than 1,000 letters seeking this opportunity. Renu, then my fiancée, gained a Japanese government sponsored scholarship and later joined me on this unlikely quest. Having no money to be married we applied to a local television program that broadcast and supported our wedding in the traditional Japanese style. Thus our life together had begun, in a foreign land, in a foreign tongue, with no roadmap and no precedents. It was the perfect beginning for a mystery or a dream.

Having mastered the Japanese language, I joined General Electric Company where my career progressed beyond my wildest imagination. Eventually I joined the Japanese Board of Directors for GE's large, global medical equipment production joint venture. I was among a very few foreigners to have achieved this status in the JV's 21 year history and I was the first Indian to ever do so. This was a reality completely unpredictable when I prematurely ended my university experience and it was possible only because I followed the Six Rules.

Today I have my own business, headquartered in Tokyo and Shanghai, bridging the cultures and technologies of Japan, China and India. My destiny has become my own to master but the dream continues.

Renu has realized an even more amazing dream. Arriving in Japan as an immigrant, unable to find a meaningful job, she built her own business. Starting first by teaching Indian cooking from our home she has become a national celebrity appearing often on television, authoring 5 books, developing her own brand of frozen foods and leading gourmet tours to India - even to a 1997 audience with Mother Teresa.

Aditya, our son, is a true 21st century internationalist; an Indian citizen, born and raised in Japan, living in the USA, working for one of the world's pre-eminent global corporations, GE. He was married to Vibha, a lovely bride on March 9th, 2003 in New Delhi, and is a father of our beautiful princess, Aarna Sakura. He is equally at home culturally and linguistically in the USA, Japan and India.

I have a dream ...

... That even the most mediocre person can achieve their fullest potential by committing to and continuously following the *Six Rules*. These are:

1. Commit to a dream ... the wilder the better.
2. Believe in yourself.
3. Try all the unconventional ideas directed by your 'night computer' (subconscious brain).
4. Make mistakes - the bigger the better - and be willing to learn so as not to repeat those mistakes.
5. Never give up ... persevere steadily and patiently.
6. Enjoy the journey.

Many people have approached me to share my 'secrets' with today's youth who have apparently lost the value of the dream. I sincerely believe that *my journey of dreams* will inspire you to initiate your own journey of dreams. For those of you who are already in the middle of your journey you will, as Gail Brook Burket wrote, "have continued courage to scale the hardest peaks and transform every stumbling block into a stepping stone".

I look forward to seeing you soon among the persons of value ... creating a positive difference in and around your world.

December 2005 **Deven Arora**
Tokyo

ACKNOWLEDGEMENTS

In writing this book a lot of inspiration should be attributed to Renu, Vibha bitia and Aditya, my lovely family with my utmost sense of gratitude.

I am particularly indebted to many people without whom this book could not have been written, but four of them are of special significance: Masahiko Agata, John Van Fleet, Stuart Walkley and Keith Williams. You will find their names dotted everywhere in this book or I should say deeply imprinted on my entire life. They have guided, motivated and supported me on every page of the book. They have gone over my manuscript word by word, yet preserving the originality of my thoughts. Therefore, I must clearly state that the final responsibility on the contents lies entirely on me.

It would be a remiss not to state as to how I came in contact with Mr. Kuldeep Jain, the Publisher. During our first meeting in Tokyo on July 16th 2005, it was an instant click. Kuldeep's immediate reaction after reading my manuscript was that it would be a difficult sell, as no one knows me in India but willing to help me give it a try.

While planning this, Dr. T.J. Bhagat of B.Jain Publishers (P) Ltd., graciously kept giving me a strong encouragement by reminding me of the uniqueness of the avenue I have walked which should be known by those who are struggling to find their ways to make break through in different circumstances in different parts of the world.

A special word of thanks goes to Christine Sas, Dutch Department, University College, London. Christine edited for clarity while preserving my Indian-English Grammar. She felt it was very exciting and good to keep in its own form as 'it reflects you and your culture'.

I am also deeply indebted to Toshifumi Tsuji, an esteemed colleague, Vivien Chang, my assistant in Stanley and Rahul Desai, a very talented young friend. They all read the manuscript and made the helpful suggestions for additions, subtractions and reorganization.

My father, Kesho Ram, had read the proof several times. He even narrated to my mother, Sushila Arora. Their distilled wisdom of 165 years combined had many valuable insights.

The inspiration for Jacket design came from Sabrina Lee. Her creative blending of the underlying theme of the book and my life is beautifully portrayed on the Cover.

On this opportunity, I deeply thank Yoriko Miyashita, Mayumi Kudo, Kyoko Fujiya, Megumi Niwa, Chiyumi Sato, Valery Chueh and Echo Cao who, being true executives themselves, have demonstrated their loyalty to and confidence in me, helping me achieve each and every step of the ladder I climbed in the course of my life with GE, Medtronic, and the Stanley as important parts of my journey to dream.

Finally, I cannot list all the people who made the life chronicled in these pages possible – all the teachers and mentors of my youth; and my friends of a lifetime. None of them are responsible for the failure of my life, but for whatever good has come out of it they deserve much of the credit. As Isaac Newton said that if I could see farther it was because I was standing on the shoulders of these Giants.

CONTENTS

1. Good-for-nothing-guy was carved into a beautiful statue 1
2. Dare to dream 4
3. Find a mentor 8
4. The power of sheer love 13
5. On the path to ruin myself 16
6. Enjoy the journey 22
7. On the 9,998th stair 26
8. Do not bring your problems ... Bring your solutions 32
9. 1,000+ letters did not go in vain 41
10. No surprise, please ! 45
11. The touch of midas 49
12. Indian couple on Japanese TV 52
13. *Kiki* (Crisis) - with hardships come creativity 56
14. Follow the leaders 61
15. Owning our properties 70
16. From 'doer' to 'leader' 85
17. Where my skills were challenged 95
18. The makings of the best global sourcing team 98
19. Delivering on 8% productivity commitment 107
20. On joining GEYMS board 117
21. Sitting on the other side of fence 122
22. Medtronic ... My second life 129
23. In the valley of abyss 139
24. An opportunity that rewrote my life 144
25. The dream continues 159
    Finale 162

CONTENTS

1. Good-for-nothing-boy masteryed into a beautiful tune 1
2. Dare to dream 4
3. Find a mentor 8
4. The power of sheer love 13
5. On the path to run myself 16
6. Enjoy the journey 22
7. On the 9,900th stair 29
8. Do not bring your problem - bring your solutions 32
9. 1000+ tests did not go in vain 41
10. Be surprised, pleased! 45
11. The touch of Midas 49
12. Indian couple on Japanese TV 52
13. With (Crisis) with madness come creativity 56
14. Follow the leader 61
15. Owning our processes 70
16. From 'doer' to 'leader' 83
17. ..... were my skills were challenged 91
18. The making of the best global sourcing team 99
19. Delivering on $ productivity commitment 107
20. From joining GEYMS found 117
21. Resting on the other side of fence 122
22. Medhanali - My second life 129
23. IN the valley of abyss 136
24. GPA opportunity that rewrote my life 140
25. The dream continues 150
    Finale 167

CHAPTER 1

GOOD-FOR-NOTHING-GUY WAS CARVED INTO A BEAUTIFUL STATUE

Trust in God. Believe in yourself. Dare to dream...
Dr. Robert Schuller

M. Scott Peck in his internationally acclaimed book 'The Road Less Traveled' states that 'life is difficult'. It is his underlying thesis that people need to understand and live amicably with the complexities of life. In my experience, life has been difficult but fair. While I do not, of course, know what the future holds in store I'm very contented, blessed and fortunate. The 57 years for Renu and 63 years of mine have been highly rewarding and enjoyable. Do not get me wrong - please! Our life has not been served to us on a silver platter. We both work almost 18 hours a day and 7 days a week. As with Thomas Edison's definition of work, 'I never did a day's work in my life. It was all fun!' In our case we both tried to like every assignment dealt to us and then molded our world to our liking.

My life began with a very conservative, God-fearing and simple family. I was born on October 6, 1942 in Meerut, India, still under British Colonial Rule and in the midst of World War II.

Until June 17, 1965 I was a mediocre college dropout, failing consecutively in more than 25 competitive tests. Still my parents kept investing in me with a fervent hope that one-day I would awaken. Indeed I owe a great debt to their confidence, pure love and financial backing. Appearing in each of those 25 entrance exams took me through every nook and corner of India like an itinerant traveler. It was exciting to visit so many good places but never a happy homecoming with the bad news of another failure. Yet, while I was in the midst of this 'dark period' I had an inexplicable tremendous confidence that my brightest future lays ahead of me. I believed in myself!

In April 1963, I felt so bad that I went to Rajkot (birth place of Mahatma Gandhiji) to take a diploma in audio engineering. While there was little prestige to be gained, it was very easy to gain admission and I was able to escape the heat at home. My parents showed little emotion at the news but their expectations were obvious ... prove yourself!

During my 2 years in Rajkot College I lived like a Maharajah while my father was toiling sweat and blood to support me. My grades were unremarkable but the satisfaction was that I did not fail. My teachers became very good friends. I actively took part in drama, the college union and served as secretary of sports; building a larger networks of friends. Away from the many constraints of home, one trait of mine became obvious ... attracting people! I didn't hone this skill until many years later but even today it keeps me in good stead.

In March, 1965 K.B. Sharma, an examiner from RCA Bombay, visited our school. On the recommendation of my principal, S.P. Taneja, Mr. Sharma agreed to provide me an internship repairing audio amplifiers. While the job was somewhat interesting it was also another excuse for me not to return to my hometown, Meerut.

After I had spent one month on the job, Mr. Sharma recommended that I visit cinematographic equipment manufacturers such as RCA and Westrex. When I met Mr. Shreeprakash Agarwal, owner of Westrex Cinecita, Bombay, he hired me on the spot. The salary of only 150 rupees was 25% less than the pocket allowance provided by my father when I was a student. This reality was my first wake-up call in life. Shocked with my circumstances but unwilling to again return home a failure, I vowed to stand on my own feet, independent from my parents, come what may. My life changed dramatically. I stayed at the Hotel Aroma where monthly charges for a bed (four beds in one room) were 80 rupees. While this was a very modest amount and humble living it consumed 53% of my total income!

Mr. Shreeprakash's older brother, S.N. Agarwal, was a self-made industrialist. He was very demanding on himself; a workaholic whose philosophy was 'work has not killed anyone - but pretending to work has taken many lives'. He was fair to his wife, brothers and employees in demanding quality work, on-time execution and delivery on commitments. He worked almost 18 hours, 7 day a week and often he would tell me that I was good for nothing, just like a stone, but promised that, if I stuck with him, he would carve me into a beautiful statue. Just as the exquisite touch of a master cutter creates value from a rough diamond Mr. S.N. Agarwal did the same during 4 years of my stay with him.

Lesson

Believe in yourself.

CHAPTER 2

DARE TO DREAM

All things are difficult before they are easy...
                                                    John Norley

My roommate at the time, Jitu Thakur, was an associate producer of 'Pramod Films'. His movie in 1965, 'Love In Tokyo' took him to Japan for almost 3 weeks for location shooting. Thereafter, living with him was nothing but hearing all good things of Japan ... day and night! He was consumed with his love for Japan. Hearing so much of Japan, my brain was totally washed out. On June 17, 1965, I made a decision to go to Japan to learn television engineering, vowing that on my return I would start my own business, manufacturing television receivers in India. The dream was cast.

THEREFORE, WHAT'S THE NEXT STEP?

I did believe in my dream ... to go to Japan to learn Television Engineering and on return ... to start my own television receivers manufacturing plant in India.

Consider, though, the odds stacked against me:
- I was just a 23-year-old lad.

- I had no connection whatsoever with Japan.
- I had no knowledge of Japanese language - neither speaking nor reading.
- I had no basic knowledge of television electronics.
- I had no passport and no visa for Japan. Neither could I leave India nor could I enter Japan.
- I had no funds.

So, even if I could land in Japan (at the boundary of the wildest stretch of my dream) how would I survive?

As you will see, that was just the tip of the iceberg.

The more I thought about it, the more reality started sinking in. I became frightened and lost the courage to share my dream with anyone. I expected that they would laugh at my absurdity, especially as my friends knew my track record.

The company you keep knows you well. Four of my best friends in 1959 were on the same 'starting line' with me. Four years later they each had significant life accomplishments;

- Ashok Mathur earned an M.A. (English Lit.) Hons. at Agra University.
- Arvind Popli rose to Lieutenant rank within the Indian military.
- Mahabir Premi gained his wings as a pilot officer in the Indian Air Force.
- Suresh Tonwar was awarded a M.Sc. (Physics) Gold Medalist, at Agra University.

Yet I was still on the same starting line wondering how and when to start the race. The fear of becoming a laughing stock of my peers, friends and relatives forced to keep my dream to myself. However, I had to move forward. The choice, otherwise, was to abandon the dream. No one forced me to commit to this dream.

No one even knew of the dream. I had the safe option to settle down to an ordinary, happy Indian life. Fortunately, the fire in me kept on calling to find ways to give it a sincere try, regardless of whatever the outcome may be. Eventually I realized that the failing was not so bad as failing to take the chance.

Step one on the road to the dream was to reinforce the self-commitment that I had made on June 17, 1965. I would re-read this 10 times whenever that I thought I was sinking down. After reading it 50 times or so, it made me hungry with a strong desire to go for it.

Step two was to find and contact The Consulate of Japan in Bombay. There, I visited their library and noted the addresses for the 40 top television manufacturing companies starting from Sony, Matsushita, Hitachi, Sanyo, Sharp, and Toshiba.

The following weekend I worked late into the night handwriting letters to each of the 40 companies. These were posted on Monday morning, costing me rupees 50 which was 33% of my monthly income.

The initial outcome was disappointing. Two weeks passed without a single response!

It appeared to me that my strategy had failed. I went back to my June 17th resolution and read it over and over again.

Frustrated with my failure, I channeled my energy and concentration into my job.

After two more weeks had passed, I said to myself, "Let me try once again." I sent 40 new letters, this time very brief notes, to the same 40 companies requesting their feedback to my request.

During this period, I also read about the activities of the Indo-Japanese Association. My sub-conscious mind was highly tuned to anything Japanese. I saw that this might advance my cause so I thought to seek their guidance and contacted Mr. Gopal Pohekar, Managing Director. His secretary spoke very nicely but told me that Mr. Pohekar was a very busy person. He had no time to meet me. Unfortunately, my second batch of letters brought no response. After almost 3 months effort I had not moved an inch forward.

Lesson

Commit to a dream. Believe you can achieve. The fire in you will keep on calling to find ways to give it a sincere try regardless of whatever the outcome may be. Eventually you will realize that the failing was not so bad as failing to take the chance.

■

CHAPTER 3

FIND A MENTOR

A single conversation across the table with a wise man is worth a month's study of books...

Chinese Proverb

No progress in 3 months.

One evening I happened to sit next to a senior colleague, Mr. R. Subramanium, while going home in the train. He asked me whether my health was okay as working for the 'Agarwals' was like toiling sweat and blood. He observed that I put in more than 13 hours every day and so it would be easy for me to be burnt out. He advised me to be careful with my health, especially as I was alone in such a big city like Bombay, and to take care. I thanked him for his soothing and kind words. He sensed, though, that something was bothering me. With a casual smile he asked whether I had a girlfriend. I said, "Not yet". He then kept quiet probably thinking that I am a bit abnormal. Before getting off the train, he asked me if I was free on the coming Sunday. If so, he wanted to invite me to his house. He knew that since I was living in a hotel, I might, perhaps be homesick. This was a rare opportunity for me to visit somebody's home. Who knows, I might even be offered a home-cooked meal. The very thought of home cooking compelled me to say 'Yes'.

For the next three days, I pondered whether it was appropriate to share my dream with Mr. Subramanium. My biggest fear was that he would laugh at my 'fantasy'. Since he has seen me in action thirteen hours daily for six months and he seemed to have a good impression of me, and I did not want to diminish that image. Only later did I come to know that he liked me for my dedication and demeanors such as respect for elders and customers. On Sunday morning, 10:00 a.m. sharp, I arrived at the Subramanium home fully equipped with my communication file.

He had a small but beautiful house. It was meticulously clean. He served me South Indian style coffee in stainless cup, it was delicious.

After I settled, he said that I seemed to be worried about something.

"Are your parents well?" "Yes", I said, "They are in the pink of health".

"Then what? Why are you not behaving like your usual cheerful and enthusiastic self?"

Like a school child who had been caught stealing something, I mustered my courage and replied, "I have to share something important. First, however, I want to make sure that you would not laugh at me, that you will keep it to yourself, and that you will help me however you can!"

Mr. Subramanium's curiosity was at its peak, "Come on. For the last 4 days you are playing hide and seek games. What are you up to?"

He listened to my dream.

He saw my letters.

Then his first comment was that no Japanese would understand me because:
- My handwriting was too difficult for them to read.
- My choice of words was too complex.
- My writing had no focus – it failed to say what I wanted.
- My letters were too long and boring.
- My usage of typical Indianized english language would be too confusing for a non-Indian.

Mr. Subramanium reminded me that as far as he understood (and he was neither an expert on Japan nor its people), english was a secondary language for Japanese people. Although they may have learnt it in school, very few people would speak or use it regularly. Therefore, my communication must be brief and to the point in order to motivate a response.

"No wonder I did not get any response," I muttered.

Mr. Subramanium requested some time to consider my plight. "Let us meet again after two weeks, same time, my home."

On the second visit his wife and daughter served me home made cuisine for lunch. It was delicious and it was free. Both were critical to my survival. On this occasion Mr. Subramanium advised me that I had to find a way to meet with Mr. Pohekar as neither Mr. Subramanium nor myself knew much about Japan, its people, culture, traditions and business organization, Mr. Pohekar would be better informed.

On Monday, I again called Mr. Pohekar's secretary. She reminded me what she had told me four weeks ago. This time I persisted in asking just five minutes of his time. Perhaps trying to get me off the phone she asked me to send her a note outlining the objectives for the meeting. Mr. Pohekar could then decide whether or not to accept an appointment.

Mr. Subramanium congratulated me on my success. "Why", I asked. "What for?" He replied that I had learned the first lesson - To reach the boss, customer or any person of influence ... 'Capture the heart of their secretary'. If you want to go through the gate then befriend the gatekeeper. I had done it!

This was my first lesson in networking and gaining access to people at the top. It was true forty years ago and it is true today. It is one of the keys of my success. In my dealings with people, I always approach the secretary first. I never go direct. Secretaries in today's organizations have so much power that they 'remote control' their bosses. The smart ones play their cards gracefully but confidently. Invariably I've become a friend and confident to all the secretaries including Presidents, CEO's and even the Deputy Prime Minister of one country. They share much more than I want to know even without even my asking. All I do is to listen carefully, keep my eyes open and avoid getting them into trouble. I applied the same lessons with the seven secretaries I had the privilege to work with in the last thirty-one years. They are as Peter Drucker said *'The Effective Executive.'*

I wrote a small note and requested Mr. Subramanium's secretary to type it. I was afraid that word would leak out in the office that I was looking for greener pastures elsewhere and that I was no longer loyal to the Agarwals. Since it was a family owned business, owners, based on their perceptions made the decisions. There are always people around you who will envy your growth or ambition and will try to keep you at their level. Backbiting is common in organizations the world over and our environment was no different. Still, it was a risk that I needed to take.

Two weeks after posting the note I called Mirdula, Mr. Pohekar's secretary. She told me in a friendly tone that Mr. Pohekar had not seen it yet. I requested her to kindly take care and she asked me to call her after a week. After 6 months effort, more than 80 letters to Japan (expending nearly a months wages on postage and paper) I still had no replies and no meeting with Mr. Pohekar. It was zero progress. Any rational person would have been dejected and defeated but I was still optimistic. Mr. Subramanium's guidance and encouragement was propelling me.

Lesson

To reach the boss, customer or any person of influence ... ' Capture the heart of their secretary'. If you want to go through the gate then befriend the gatekeeper.

CHAPTER 4

THE POWER OF SHEER LOVE

Where there is love there is life...
Mahatma Gandhi

Bombay is the financial capital of India. Its population was then around 8 million. The cities where I was born, educated and spent my first 23 years were Meerut and Rajkot. These cities were very small (population not exceeding 100,000 each) so my parents were concerned about my safety and well being living in Bombay. Therefore, they looked around for someone in our town among our near and distant relations and friends to find an introduction for me in Bombay. This was to be a lifeline in the event that I need some help. A relative, Mrs. Sushila Arora (Mr. K.L. Arora's daughter), was settled there. A letter of introduction was posted and I was given a copy, which I promptly misplaced, hence I could not establish contact. Actually, I did not feel the need also. However, Mrs. Sushila Arora's family in Bombay felt it strange to have no contact with me. They wrote back to their family in Meerut that this guy has not bothered to even call. My *Mummiji* (mother) reminded me to touch base with them as soon as possible.

On the following Sunday, Babbu, a very dear cousin of mine and a top scholar studying Mechanical Engineering in Poona, came to Aroma and we both decided to visit Mrs. Sushila Arora's home together. That was Renu's house. She was just 16 then. Babbu and I both had a great time - delicious food in a warm homely atmosphere, with a wonderful family. When we left their home late that evening, they came to see us off till the gate. Talking later that evening, Renu's *Mummiji* (mother) and *Papaji* (father) discovered that they had the same thought on their mind. Mummiji asked Papaji as to what he thought of me as a potential candidate for Renu's husband. Papaji shot back with surprise as to how did she come to know that he was thinking of the same thing that moment. This is the Indian way of matchmaking. Marriages are made in Heaven but neither Renu nor I had any clue.

Mummiji was very special. She was the spring of eternal love! Sometimes I misinterpreted her love and dedication for me and I complained about it to my own parents but my Mummiji (mother) corrected me all the times. Mummiji was very inquisitive about me: what I am, what I aspire to become in my life, what was my past - every thing! Although she was not highly educated she understood what I was up to. I was reluctant to share my past and the dream I held for the future. She so loved me and I did not want to go down in her esteem. I feared that if she came to know me fully she would not like to see me again. She was almost a goddess to me and I did not want to lose my credibility with her, but I was absolutely wrong. She did not care about my past, my weaknesses, stupidities, and foibles. She accepted me exactly as I was - with my poor educational background, low salary but with some strengths too - a total package.

One Sunday afternoon, in private, I mustered my courage and told her my dream. I was expecting her to chop me down, bring my feet down to the earth and remind me of the reality of life with comments like... "Do not fly in the air, look at your track record. Be realistic and do not think of the moon while you have difficulty of walking straight on the ground."

However, nothing of this sort happened!

She quietly listened to everything and did not speak a single word during the 30 minutes of my talk. I was perspiring and so nervous. When I finished she simply kissed my cheeks. Her eyes told me everything ... she was very proud of me! From her eternal love all my facades started melting down and I started turning into a small kid. This is the power of sheer love, which started gradually transforming my life!

Lesson

Love is the energizer.

CHAPTER 5

ON THE PATH TO RUIN MYSELF

*Do not wish to be any thing but what you are,
and try to be that perfectly...*

St. Francis De Sales

With Mummiji's love as my energizer, I would started assuming more responsibilities in my work and my salary doubled to 300 rupees. Mr. Shreeprakash Agarwal, the youngest brother of S.N. had a special liking for me. I spent 80% of my time with him doing his errands and meeting with the customers. He started relying more on me. From this came power.

I ran the entire office, staying for 14 hours every day including weekends, attending to customers, negotiating and concluding the deals, taking them out for demonstrations, responding to sales enquiries and complaints. I had an excellent team and people were very friendly to me. While the work was hard we had fun as well, like having lunch or spending tea time together.

I was very poor in dictating business letters. Whatever I dictated, Lydia D'Costa, the office secretary, would type a letter which conveying what I wanted –but had failed - to convey. Her english skills, spoken and written, were excellent. All I had to do was to sign my name. I was very grateful that Lydia was quietly covering my weakness.

As the sailing in the office was smooth, S.N. felt that we were not working hard enough or delivering on our full potential. He had a habit of shouting at the people and he never seemed to be satisfied with whatever output you delivered. The phrase, '*good enough*' was not in his vocabulary. From his continuous pressure, I also picked up the habit of shouting at my staff and I started speaking at the top of my voice. Only our customers were spared. All I did was shouting, shouting ... and nothing but shouting even if I only needed a glass of water.

After a few weeks I noted some change in my team's behavior. They started keeping their distance from me. They responded politely and to the point on the demands I made to them but the friendly and warm atmosphere had turned chilled and silent. When I tried to join them during lunch they invariably found an excuse to leave me alone. After three months had passed, it looked as though I was choking. The pressure of work was monumental. S.N. started shouting more because work had slowed down. In turn I started shouting more. Often I would be in the office until 2 a.m. S.N. questioned Shreeprakash's judgment in assigning this responsibility to an unqualified 'Deven'. S.N. recommended that I be fired, as I was a sick person. I asked myself why, when S.N. shouts at the staff it is no issue but when I did the same it destroyed the morale. All I had been doing is following his example and philosophy of keeping the labor under your boots.

My job was no longer fun.

I sought help from my many friends and well-wishers. My choice was to leave or be fired. I was not in the mood to leave and definitely did not want to be fired so I thought of seeking Pitaji's (my father) counsel. His distilled wisdom, written back to me in his own hand, is vividly etched in my brain:

> '*Inder, success has gone to your head! You're on the path to ruin yourself!! People listen to Mr. S.N. because they have no choice. He controls their purse and therefore their destiny, whereas you're perceived as being bought by him because you got higher salary and status. Unless you learn to maintain yourself cool, stop swearing and shouting, you'll be fired very soon. People love you for what you are. They will never let you down if you bring back your lively demeanors.*'

This golden advice is still my hallmark today. I must confess that maintaining my self-control is still the most difficult thing to do, but this counsel brought my feet back to the ground. After nearly 3 months I began to regain the team's confidence.

In February 1966, I again called Mirdula to seek an appointment with Mr. Pohekar. Although Mr. Pohekar was very busy he agreed to allow some time in the first week of March. In a very friendly tone she advised, "Call me again around February end. I should be able to fine-tune the appointment time then!"

On February 27th I called again. 'Mr. Pohekar can see you on March 4th at 5 p.m. Come around 16:55. Don't be late'.

I arrived at Mr. Pohekar's office at 4:45 p.m. This was the first time I met Mirdula. I took my communication file containing the more than 80 letters. As I waited I had the impression that, on this particular day, Mr. Pohekar had many visitors. Later on I came to know that a continuous stream of guests was the norm.

With the flow of incoming and outgoing visitors, it appeared to me that I might not have a chance to meet with him at all. However, Mirdula assured me that he would definitely see me because he knew I had been trying to reach him for the last four months. Mr. Pohekar was curious to meet a person of my patience and mission. 5:00 p.m. passed and no call. At 5:30 she told me that he was talking with the Consulate-General of Japan on phone and I must continue waiting outside his office until I was called in. 9:00 p.m., still no call. No one was inside his office and no one was waiting outside other than myself. I thought that he had completely forgotten about me and wondered what I should I do. Should I continue sitting patiently or should I knock on his door? Finally, at 9:15 p.m., I ventured and knocked. He called me in and asked my name. "Okay, just continue sitting outside for a few more minutes. As soon as I have finished the task at hand I will call you. I am in the middle of something urgent and important." The reply was terse but delivered with a smile.

Finally, at 9:45 p.m. I was called in. Mr. Pohekar said he had a dinner appointment at 10:00. Unless he was to be awfully late for the dinner he could only afford me 5 minutes. I had to tell him what I wanted quickly and so I started as fast as I could.

I gave him my communication file to look at. He started glancing at the letters and after turning 4 or 5 pages he interrupted me saying, "These letters will never fetch a reply from Japanese people since they are not accustomed to writing letters. They are not prolific communicators like we Indians. They have a different form of communication which gets them along inside or outside of Japan." He had no time to explain further and suggested that I see him again after two weeks at which time he would give me a few contact names to address. With these new contacts I had permission to use his name as a reference! Further, he said that it would be ideal to write a formal introduction letter from him because Japanese people are very conservative. Since he has no time, this work was left to me.

F3

I thanked him profusely for a very encouraging and supportive meeting. This was my first positive step in 8 months and there was some hope to move forward in a direction with discipline. During my five hours waiting outside of his office on a steel chair, I had been cursing him that he asked me to come at 4:55 p.m. sharp and then kept me outside for so long. After the meeting, all my ill feelings turned into gratitude because he was confident to let his name be used by me (who met him for just 5 minutes) to his well-placed friends. I was on cloud nine!

The next day I informed Mr. Subramanium. He said, "your aspirations are like scaling Mt. Everest and this was the first step in that direction." Since Mr. Pohekar was a very busy person Mr. Subramanium recommended that we could draft the covering letters on his behalf. If he approved the letter, all Mr. Pohekar would need to do is provide his signature. I also called Mirdula to thank her for making it possible to meet Mr. Pohekar. She asked me to brief her with the details and I did so. She felt great! I asked her about the possibility of our drafting letters of introduction on Mr. Pohekar's behalf. She promised to consult with him and that she would have an answer for me when I called her again for the follow-up meeting in two weeks. Meanwhile, Mr. Subramanium gave me a template of letters to be written. It focused on a brief self-introduction, my vision or dream, and a description of help or support I was requesting. It was a precise and concise format. He asked me to get these letters typed and I requested a colleague of his, Chandra Shekharan, to type them for me with a fervent hope that Agarwals would not discover my 'side business'. Chandra promised to maintain the confidentiality and kept his promise for the next three years.

With the 40 letters in-hand and a template for the covering letter, I approached Mirdula for the next appointment. Again, I was told to visit him at 5:00 p.m. I was praying in my heart that I would not face another five hour wait outside his office. Well, this time I was ushered in at 8:30 p.m. – one hour less waiting than my first visit which was some small progress.

I showed him my updated letters and the draft of covering letter. He liked everything and asked only one question, 'Who is the brain behind such laser crisp letters since it obviously is not you?' My response was, "Of course I am fortunate to be mentored by a senior colleague of mine, Mr. Subramanium." Mr. Pohekar gave me 5 names, their addresses and his private letterhead. These 5 persons were the head of a Buddhist sect, a parliamentarian, a professor at Tokyo University, and business division managers in Toshiba and Sony - an entire cross-section of elite leaders. In the following week, I delivered 5 letters for his signature and one blank which he told me that I might need as a contingency. Mirdula asked me to return a week later to collect the signed documents. Meanwhile, I posted my 40 own letters. Mr. Pohekar's signed letters were in mail a week later.

Now I had posted 125 letters to Japan but I felt that real progress was being made.

Lesson

'Success should not go to head! Learn to maintain cool. People love you for what you are. They will never let you down if you continue your lively demeanors.'

∎

CHAPTER 6

ENJOY THE JOURNEY

Success is a journey, not a destination...
Ben Sweetland

April 7th, 1966 was a red-letter day in my life. On that day I received my first communication from Japan! It was a letter from Mr. Kenichiro Komai, President, Hitachi, Ltd., Tokyo. In 1966 Hitachi was ranked amongst the Top Ten of Fortune 500 Companies. To me it was like winning gold in the Olympic games. I was so excited on touching the envelope itself that I did not want to open it, and damage the contents. Just by having received a letter from a person of Mr. Komai's stature, I was elated and I felt as if I had achieved my mission in life. Jitu Thakur, my roommate who 'brain washed' me to go to Japan, reminded me to read the contents. Although he did not say it, his tone implied it might not be the panacea of my aspirations. Gradually, with utmost care, I opened the letter, as I did not want to miss anything. It was a very short letter.

Dear Mr. Arora:

I am favorably impressed with your vision, drive and aspirations you hold for your country. These are indeed laudable.

However, the reality is that Hitachi being a legal business entity, it cannot enter with any individual like you into a business agreement for obvious reasons.

Therefore, while we do very much like to help you in achieving your vision but with the circumstances stated above, I will not be of much help.

It's my opinion that you sharpen your focus since television is a vast field ... like Broadcasting, Manufacturing of Television Receivers, etc. You can spend whole of your life in just one particular discipline.

I wish you very best and sincerely regret in dashing your hopes, whatever you might have had from Hitachi. Since you are a young dynamic person, I am sure, you would find other avenues to canalize your enthusiasm.

In conclusion, I am compelled to write to you because I admire your persistence. I am in receipt of 3 excellent letters from you. However, I would appreciate no more communication, please!

Sincerely

Kenichiro Komai,
President.

I read that letter more than 100 times. I did not know what to do next. I was so numb as if my entire energy had drained out of my body. I lay down on the bed and slept without dinner or changing my clothes. I woke up the next morning still fully clothed, even wearing my shoes.

At office, I showed that letter to Mr. Subramanium. To me it was a stark reality of immaturity (mine) and maturity (Mr. Subramanium). After reading the letter he said,

'In order to reach the goal you have set your heart on there are 9,999 stairs to climb. Each step will bring some progress and will bring you closer to your goal. Therefore, enjoy the journey. Think positively and stop worrying that every letter you wrote should bring 'Yes' to your request. Keep your eyes and ears open. Look for opportunities. Listen to people. Think pros and cons and act on what you believe is right. And again enjoy the journey, because the journey is as important as the goal'.

Thereafter, my attitude was different. I stopped worrying about the responses to the 125 letters. I just kept writing and vowed to continue seeking Japanese opportunities.

Over the next three years I mailed more than 1,000 letters! It was a case of 98% one-sided communication. It became fun and I tried everything without regret for the time and postage consumed. I was in action. In fact, action has always been my forte!

The whole process taught me many valuable lessons:

- *Networking: By making many friends in Japan and in India my network grew by leaps and bounds. Without this network my dream could never have become reality.*

- *Ownership: From this process I became a professional on Japan. People would inquire about Japan - its culture, business, history and life style – and I could answer anything. Having that knowledge about where I was going allowed me to succeed when I arrived.*

- *Communication: Not only did I learn how to communicate clearly and succinctly in English I also started learning the Japanese language.*

- *Persistence: Many people criticized me for dividing my focus and spending more than 50% of my salary on Japan-related projects. They wondered how long it would continue and whether four years might not be enough. They believed that if I concentrated on my job I would have much more progress. Fortunately, my parents were solidly behind me. Mummiji's (Renu's mother) continuous encouragement was an essential driver.*

- *Competition: I have reasons to believe that 'Agarwals' knew of my aspirations. Neither did they discourage me nor did they interfere. Apparently, they were satisfied with my contribution to their business. One Sunday morning I was with S.N. and he asked me when I would settle down in life, get married and have family? I could not believe my ears. In almost 40 months of service it was my very first exposure on personal level. That day lady luck smiled and he gave me a handsome raise. My Salary was 600 rupees per month. He wanted me to stay, not go to Japan.*

CHAPTER 7

ON THE 9,998TH STAIR

The people who get on in this world are the people who get up and look for the circumstances they want, and, if they can't find them, make them...
George Bernard Shaw

While I was marching forward on my journey, pressure was mounting on me to think about married life and to stop living out of a suitcase. Mummiji and Pitaji asked me in late 1966 as to what I thought of Renu as my life partner (had they conspired with SN?). I replied that this was perfectly okay with me if Renu would also agree. My only request was to hold the marriage until I return after having lived in Japan for one year. Their next question then was, "What's the timeline?" The implication was that, since I did not have a firm itinerary established yet, I could get married and still keep on trying my quest. My fear was that once I got married, my whole focus would then shift to taking care of my family ... reality vs. what I wanted to do – keeping fantasy!

Pitaji came to my rescue again. He asked if I could set a future date for marriage independent of success regarding my Japan goal. "Yes", I said "3 years from now (until 1969) regardless of the outcome." Seeking my commitment, Mummiji (Renu's Mom) desired to get us engaged in 1966. I spoke of my fear with Pitaji that once I am engaged I will be dragged down into marriage much before 1969. He guided me with golden words, reflecting his progressive outlook and forward thinking. It was what we used to see in Indian movies, but with some modifications. He guided me by clearly sorting out the issues. With this engagement I would know my life partner, Renu. I would have a firm commitment to marry in 1969. Further, I would live in Bombay. This meant that I could utilize this great opportunity to know Renu better and let her know me. We could understand each other's backgrounds; share our likings, disliking, and our future aspirations. She could even become my partner in my quest for Japan; contributing with her very fertile brain. That's exactly how it happened.

Papaji, Mr. B.M. Arora, had the best network I know of. One of his favorite activities was to invite people to their home for lunch, dinner, or even breakfast. He would go to any extent to help people in connecting them, exploring ways to help them getting their things done. He was a man of very many contacts, and he always followed up, never leaving any stone unturned. He always planned ahead. His attention to details and execution skills were excellent! He was always eager to provide me new leads and he introduced me to many persons who had links to Japan or were in a position to recommend one. Japan was still very mysterious and the least understood country in those days. People used to tell me that atomic fall-outs were still very common in Hiroshima and Nagasaki during the rainy season and the first thing you lose was your hair. Surprisingly, there were not so many Japan experts then.

One day I was called for dinner and there I was introduced to one Mr. Pathekar. He was an officer with Reserve Bank of India. Among the many functions of RBI they controlled foreign exchange and had the final say in granting the permission to go abroad.

Mr. Pathekar told me that if I could find some educational institution, preferably of television engineering, in Japan that would be willing to admit me, he would be able to help me. Since I had developed friendship with many people in Japan and India I asked around. Through Mr. Pohekar's contact, Mr. Hideo Nakajima, I came to know of Chiyoda Television Engineering Institute, Ueno, Tokyo. I requested Nakajima-san to help me in getting the admission. He was gracious to get me the admission for fall of 1968 class and he even paid the fee from his own pocket. With this document in my hand, I needed only a passport, RBI's permission, foreign exchange and visa for Japan.

The first battle was to obtain a passport in Bombay.

I was not qualified.

Period.

As I was born and raised in Meerut, Uttar Pradesh I was required to go back and process my application there. I could not apply by mail and I was told that no one knows how long it would take. It might take one year.

The idea of going back to my hometown did not appeal to me. Moreover, I had a better network in Bombay. The probability of quickly getting a passport through this network seemed better. I spoke to another colleague of mine, Bismarck Lobo, who coordinated governmental relations for Agarwals. He assured me that he could be of substantial help. With my, "Please do", he set about the task. I virtually chased his shadow for almost two weeks. He pleaded with people as if he was seeking this favor for himself. Every department and every person constantly reminded us that since I was not a resident of Bombay it would be very difficult to get the passport issued in Bombay.

Lobo's sincere efforts started yielding some dividends as he made it a point to tell everyone how far I had come in my efforts to go to Japan. Some of his friends gradually started recommending ways of making this happen. They asked me to submit my application and mentioned that it might take 6 months to get the passport. The last hurdle was to obtain a report from the local police station showing that I was a law-abiding citizen of Bombay.

No local Bombay police station had my family registry. The only avenue was to refer to my hometown in Meerut for the report. If I could get this clearance they would release my application. No one could hazard a guess when, if ever, the Meerut police report would come. Again Mr. Lobo's persuasive skills came into play. He proposed that he would personally vouch for my conduct of the past and, if something inaccurate were found, he would be responsible. He sought the favor of his very good friend who was the Deputy Superintendent of Police. The police officer told Lobo to countersign my application, which he did without a moment's hesitation. The police then released my track record with their stamp on it. I got the passport in 6 weeks time, just because of Mr. Lobo.

The second battle was with the Reserve Bank of India. With college admission documents received from Japan, and a passport, I made the application. It was rejected instantly.

Why?

I did not hold a degree from any reputable Indian college or university. The government of India could not allocate the precious foreign exchange to a non-qualified person like me. Period!

I tried to talk to many officials. My argument was on the grounds that no higher education was available in India for the discipline of television engineering. However, the field was of national interest due to the potential industrial value. Therefore, I must be granted permission. Japan was number one in this technology and on my return the whole country would be benefited.

One or two officers sympathized with me. They told that they really wanted to help me but 'the law is the law'. They were vested with no powers to bend or waive in my favor.

I did not like the attitude of RBI people. They just applied a cookie-cutter approach without looking deeper into my case's exceptional nature. I went back to Mr. Subramanium. I told him that I believed that I was standing on the 9,998th step and the last looks so far the biggest and the toughest one to climb. Mr. Subramanium had been with me through thick and thin for almost 3 years. I had never seen him so livid. As soon as he heard RBI's official line of rejection he directed me to approach the highest concerned authority in the land, H.E. Mr. Morarji Desai, Deputy Prime Minister and Minister of Finance. He said there is no risk he can say 'No'.

Mr. Subramanium drafted a very persuasive cable to be sent to H.E. Mr. Morarji Desai. The post office people looked at me from top to bottom. They looked like they wanted to quiz me as to whether I knew what I was doing. They even asked me to confirm that the recipient's name had no mistake. I assured them that this was my intention. One person commented that I looked like of 25-26 years of age and I was talking to the future Prime Minister of India. He admired my courage.

Unfortunately Mr. Desai did say 'No'! His secretary's response was to repeat the official line, which I heard from RBI's officers in Bombay. "It is the rule! It is the prevailing law!! No exception!!!"

Papaji called Mr. Pathekar a few days later. Mr. Pathekar told him that he had done some research and had discovered a bylaw: The RBI allows even non-degree holders to go overseas for specialized on-the-job training if it is not available in India. He believed that television manufacturing fell into this category. He suggested I should seek sponsorship from a company like Hitachi. I wrote a letter to Mr. Kenichro Komai, President, Hitachi, Ltd. Mr. Komai quickly responded that he could not sponsor me from India but if I could manage to come to Japan he might consider doing something... but no promise! Mr. Pathekar said that would not be acceptable.

Back to square one.

Lesson

But Never Give Up!

CHAPTER 8

DO NOT BRING YOUR PROBLEMS... BRING YOUR SOLUTIONS...

Chance favors the prepared mind...
Louis Pasteur

In 1968, there was a very hotly contested parliamentary election between two personalities of which Mr. S. K. Patil was one. Mr. Patil was a nationally recognized leader, a dedicated freedom fighter and a close disciple of Gandhiji. He had a powerful personality and his influence was to the extent that he was regarded a candidate for Prime Minister of India. Some people even called him the 'King of BPCC (Bombay Pradesh Congress Committee)'. His being the winner of that election was a foregone conclusion. However, something unthinkable happened: Mr. Patil lost the election!

In early 1969, I read in the newspaper that Patil had initiated a movement to be in touch with the grassroots again; a touch he apparently had lost during the years he was riding the crest of highest power. He opened his door to common people one morning each week. It turned out to be a very popular session. People started flocking to his home to air their grievances and seek help. He listened very patiently to every one. His secretary, Mr. Fernandez, took notes. It was, indeed, a very crowded gathering.

One Thursday morning I went to get a flavor for the event. It was an enormous challenge to get my voice heard because there were so many people and some appeared to be very influential. Later, I went to see Mr. Fernandez without an appointment but he declined to see me. It was disappointing but understandable that if he started meeting with every Tom, Dick and Harry, he would not be able to do his job. After a few days, I mailed a note to Mr. Fernandez asking him to grant me 5 minutes. I followed it with a telephone call. He did not take my call but the lady who did suggested, "The best timing to call Mr. Fernandez is at 8:00 a.m. He is an early bird." The next day at 8:00 a.m. I called and, yes, he took my call. He listened to my request but declined to arrange an audience with Mr. Patil. His explanation was Mr. Patil could not afford to meet everyone and that is the reason he came up with the brilliant idea to have Thursday morning public session. Mr. Fernandez encouraged me to come on any Thursday. According to his advice, the following Thursday, I did go at 8:00 a.m.

Mr. Patil customarily arrived at 9:30. To my surprise, there was a long queue already waiting at 8:00. Unknown to me the format of the meeting had changed. In order to enhance the effectiveness and individual's privacy, he had started meeting with one person or a family at a time. The maximum time allotted was 10 minutes per person/group. This brought discipline and efficiency but the downside was that not more than 25-30 people could meet with him per week. Every week there were more than 100 persons waiting. I did not know as to when, if ever, would I make it.

After 3 weeks of unsuccessful attempts, I approached Mr. Fernandez again. He did feel sorry for me and asked me to call him, following week. He reinforced that he was not offering any hope - it has got to be Mr. Patil's decision whether or not to see me. At the appointed time I called him. He told me, "Mr. Patil had the flu last week. He is resting. Give him another week." His tone had started becoming friendly. The next week's call brought the news that Mr. Patil would give me 5 minutes on February 28th. "You must be in his office 8:55 am. Don't be late! Come prepared and be concise."

For the next 4 days I was very excited. It was my first-ever opportunity to meet a national leader face-to-face, and that too in private! I did not share this news with anyone including Renu, Mummiji or Mr. Subramanium. Monday, 8:30 a.m. I arrived at Mr. Patil's office. I was very nervous. Mr. Fernandez saw my face and tried to cool me down by offering a glass of water. At 8:53 I entered in Mr. Patil's office. My pulse rate seemed to be 1,000 beats per minute. The office was very simple but elegant. Mr. Patil was sitting on a Gaddi (Indian style sofa). Behind him was the large portrait of Gandhiji. On two sides were equally large pictures of him ... one with Gandhiji and the other one was with Jawaharlal Nehru. Also, Gandhiji's two handwritten letters addressed to him were framed.

As soon as I entered, he looked at me with piercing eyes and I got scared. Apparently, he had been briefed. He greeted me with a question: 'Why did you come to me? I am not even an MP (Member of Parliament). Go to Indira Gandhi (then Prime Minister of India) and seek her help'. My brain stopped working. All this happened when I was still standing at the door. Tears, all of a sudden, started rolling down my face. Mr. Patil looked at me quizzically and apparently recognized my state of affairs. Shaken to my core I had the presence to remember, however, that I had been given only 5 minutes. To me it seemed that nearly 15 minutes had already passed. It is like Einstein's 'Theory of Relativity' which he explained to Sophia Loren in simple terms - that time flies when you are with a person you are in love with, but if you are on a hot burner even one second seems too long. I thought my time was up and I opened the door to go out. This action of mine made him even more upset. I was asked to sit on a sofa near him. He asked me what I wanted from him. In this emotionally distraught environment I started briefing him about my efforts of last three and half years and tried to show my communication file. He did not look at anything and cut me short with only 4 sentences:

"Do not bring your problems to me. Think of three feasible solutions to select from. I can not do thinking for you. That is your job. When you are ready... come and see me again.'

It became the key management lesson of my life. And that was one of his secrets to attain the leadership of national stature.

I brainstormed with Mr. Subramanium and Mr. Pohekar. Luckily I came across an article in the newspaper that Waco Radio Electronics Co. has a technical know-how arrangement with NEC, Tokyo. I was guided to go for a two-prong approach: One, request Mr. S.K. Patil to speak to Mr. B.N. Adarkar, then Deputy Governor RBI, to revisit my application on the ground that training in television engineering was not available in India and it is in the national interest to develop engineers in this discipline. Two, request Mr. S.C. Israni, President, Waco Radio Electronics Co. to get a letter of invitation from NEC to accept me as the on-the-job-trainee for six months in their manufacturing facilities. Mr. Israni was an active leader of Congress and therefore was closely associated with Mr. Patil.

Mr. Subramanium helped me draft these two letters. I delivered these to Mr. Fernandes so that he could check the contents. He made a few changes and asked me to bring the cleaned-up copies. The following day I delivered the final copies to Mr.

Fernandez. He asked me to call him a few days later but something happened which caused Mr. Patil to summon him into his office. As I was moving out, Mr. Fernandez came out gushingly. He told me that Mr. Patil wants to see me immediately. I was scared but went along. Mr. Patil asked me to sit down and offered me a cold drink. He admired my persistence, quick follow-up and fast learning. He dictated letters to Mr. Adarkar and Mr. Israni as per my recommendation. Within 20 minutes two white sealed envelopes were given to me - one for Mr. Adarkar and the other for Mr. Israni - with instruction to seek appointments and deliver these letters personally. I was overwhelmed by his speed and I thanked Mr. Patil from the bottom of my heart. He wished me good luck and asked me to stay in touch, which I did until his death.

I wasted no time. Immediately, from Mr. Patil's office, I contacted Mr. Adarkar's secretary. With great pride and confidence, I told him that I was carrying a letter from Mr. Patil to be delivered to Mr. Adarkar. The secretary asked me to wait on line. In less than two minutes he told me that Mr. Adarkar could see me any time at my convenience - even the afternoon of the same day would be okay. Imagine, the Deputy Governor of RBI (and future Governor) is basing his entire schedule on my convenience. I had never been used to this kind of behavior. Normally, there were 8-10 screens between me and Mr. Adarkar; peons, clerks, junior officers, senior officers, secretaries, etc., and you have to wait on each of them before you could think of seeing Mr. Adarkar. However, I was carrying Mr. Patil's glow behind my head. It was like walking in the park. I explored the possibility of next day's morning availability. To my astonishment within less than 2 minutes I was told that Mr. Adarkar would see me at 9:15 a.m.

As soon as I arrived at RBI the following day, I was led to Mr. Adarkar's chamber. No one asked any questions. It was a great feeling that I had a free (or Patil) pass. With all I had been subjected to for three and a half years it was indeed refreshing and reassuring that my efforts had not gone in vain. After a brief introduction, I delivered Mr. Patil's letter to Mr. Adarkar. To my greatest surprise, my file was on his desk. Right in front of me, he asked two senior officers to join in. He gave them the challenge ... how can we help this young man in achieving his goal? The officers' fear was that my case had been elevated to Mr. Morarji Desai's office in New Delhi and that my request had been denied. Unless they had something new and solid to qualify, howsoever sympathetic they could be, approving my application might get them into trouble.

Mr. Adarkar was not impressed with their logic. His posture was that we had got to find a way to develop leaders in areas where there is no effective expertise available in the country today. He looked at me for another alternative. I brought to his attention a bylaw stipulated by RBI which Mr. Pathekar had told me about permitting those who do not have degree to go overseas on on-the-job-training. I showed him Mr. Komai's letter. Everyone read it: but Mr. Adarkar with special interest. He felt that if I could fetch a personal response from the president of Hitachi, Ltd., I ought to possess some foresight, vision and determination to see it through. Therefore, he proclaimed that we owe to this young man within the framework of laws of the land all the encouragement he deserves. I told him about S.C. Israni's envelope which Mr. Patil wrote requesting him to get me a letter from NEC accepting me for OJT (On-The-Job-Trainee). Mr. Adarkar's face brightened up. His reaction was, "Did I want him to speak to Mr. Israni?"

Events were unraveling so fast that I could not even grasp reality. The best brains of RBI did not only want to help me but eager to go out of their way. Mr. Adarkar recognized my confusion. He guided me to meet with Mr. Israni and deliver Mr. Patil's letter. If Mr. Israni had some questions then I should direct him to call

Mr. Adarkar. Further, I should call Mr. Adarkar as soon as I had a letter from NEC. At that time he would see that RBI's clearance and necessary stipend in foreign exchange was granted immediately. He further encouraged me that, if for some unforeseen reasons either Mr. Israni or NEC refused to issue the necessary document I should visit him again and he would work with me to find another avenue. Mr. Adarkar seemed to be as enthusiastic in seeing my mission accomplished as I was. I was on cloud nine. My three and half years of journey, looking back, appeared to be so light and rewarding. It reaffirmed my faith in the value of powerful connections.

The next day I approached Mr. Israni's secretary telling her I was carrying Mr. Patil's letter. She straightaway connected me to Mr. Israni. He asked me to visit him any time of my convenience. Neither was I used to such expressions nor did leaders treat me with so much importance. It was the free usage of Mr. Patil's name, which was doing all the wonders.

I requested to meet him the same afternoon. Mr. Israni, immediately called Mr. Hattori, Division Manager, NEC, in Tokyo. Mr. Hattori was concerned about their liability but agreed to trust Mr. Israni's judgment. Mr. Israni assured him that it was a formality to obtain RBI's clearance and that I would meet my own expenses. Mr. Hattori requested the proforma invitation letter. Upon receipt, he would have it typed on NEC letterhead and mailed back with his signature. Mr. Israni telexed him the contents of the proposed letter. Later he called him again to confirm that Mr. Hattori did receive the telex. Mr. Hattori told Mr. Israni that he had already sent the letter through registered express mail (the fastest mode available then). The letter was delivered to me on the 5th day and I immediately took it to Mr. Adarkar. Clearance was granted and I was then entitled to a stipend of 500 Sterling pounds. It was Mr. Patil's magic wand that worked.

Next came the arrangement of funds. Pitaji offered me the cash of Rs. 8,000, covering the airfare and stipend 500 pounds. While I respected Pitaji's wish, I made up my mind to stand on my own feet. Renu supported me. Therefore, with great humility, I declined and instead I approached R.D. Sethna Trust, which granted scholarships to overseas students. Papaji knew the Trust's secretary-general, Mr. F.J. Anthia. Mr. Anthia responded positively and considered my application favorably. Within two weeks time, I was granted a scholarship of Rs. 7,500.

As I had many good friends in the Japanese Consulate, Bombay, my visa was issued in less than 30 minutes. It was the easiest step on the entire journey. With my passport, a Japanese visa, an Air India ticket to Osaka, RBI clearance and 430 Sterling pounds in hand, I was ready to fly to the Land of 'The Rising Sun'. It was June 14th, 1969. Pitaji and Mummiji worked with Panditji to determine the auspicious day to travel to Osaka. August 23rd, 1969 was declared the best day to fly to the east.

The next 10 weeks were a golden period of my early life. I was a high profile person. Wherever Renu and myself went and whomever we met with, we were treated like royalty. The Agarwals were proud to see that their institution has produced a person who was moving to Japan. They were very generous. They also provided many contacts should I ever have need. Pitaji wrote a letter of thanks to Mr. S.N. for grooming me for bigger challenges ahead in life. Mrs. S.N. Agarwal was deeply touched with Pitaji's fine gesture to the extent that tears rolled down. It is my firm belief that Agrawals laid the foundation of my glorious career of next thirty years.

Renu and myself were engaged on August 15th, 1969. More than 600 near and dear relatives, friends and well-wishers gathered to bless us. It was a landmark event of our lives and was made even more memorable by my lovely 4-year-old sister-in-law, Gargi. When I started to sit on 'Gaddi' my tight trouser split along the back. Gargi made this known to every one in her very imitable style. She thought that this 'hot news' was to break. Sure enough, by the time ceremony was over almost every guest knew.

On August 23rd morning, I left for Osaka. More than 100 persons saw me off at the airport – including my lovely Renu.

Lesson

"Don't discuss your problems in public. Think of three feasible solutions to select from. No body can do thinking for you. That's your job. People can help you to select from."

■

CHAPTER 9

1,000+ LETTERS DID NOT GO IN VAIN

Accept the challenges, so that you may feel the exhilaration of victory...

General George S. Patton

After staying overnight in Hong Kong, I landed on August 24th at the Itami International Airport, Osaka. It was a bright sunny day with cool breeze. With my first step on Japanese soil I experienced a feeling of warmth and welcome; a surreal emotional mix and I could not believe it was my first ever exposure to a foreign country. Strange to say... it was like homecoming. After a short taxi ride, I arrived at the International Students Dorm (*Kokusai Gakuyu Kaikan*), the place I had been directed to stay. Among many foreign nationals, there were four Indians. Therefore, it became a soft-landing.

When I was preparing to go to Japan, Mr. and Mrs. S.C. Israni invited Renu and myself to dinner. During the dinner, he casually asked whether anyone would provide support on my landing in Osaka. His concern was whether I had lined up some people to take care of me during the first week of arrival. I said I would survive somehow. He answered that in a foreign land where I did not speak their language it might be a good idea to count on someone - just in case. He then offered his very close friend, Mr. Hiroshi Yokota's name. He called him right away and made a personal request. Mr. Yokota, although very late in the night, was kind enough to accept Mr. Israni's request. He advised that I should contact him as soon as I arrived in Osaka.

On August 25th, I called on Mr. Yokota who was to become my Godfather. He ran his own small trading company. He and Mrs. Yokota were very fine persons and they gave me excellent care. Mr. Yokota took me to many places with an objective to find an institution that not only could train me in the field of television receivers manufacturing but also could help with the cultural transition to Japan's language, etiquette and other nuances. Eventually one of Yokota-san's colleagues recommended that I enroll at *Kaigai Gijutsusha Kenshu Kyokai* (Association for Overseas Technical Scholarship, AOTS). Japan's influential Ministry of International Trade and Industry (MITI) sponsored this institution bestowing it with much prestige and ability. Its objective was to promote the technological prowess of the world's number two economic power by training young engineers from developing countries of Asia, Africa, and South America. The maximum enrollment period was two years. Students received a monthly stipend of Yen 89,000. Upon completing their training, the engineers were to return home, transferring their knowledge to develop and grow their home countries. MITI also expected that these young leaders would create closer cooperation with Japan.

Yokota-san thought that AOTS would be ideal for me and he worked very hard to get me enrolled. He took on my burden by sponsoring me through his company: Koyo Trading Co., Ltd. My next step was to find a company that would train me in assembling television receivers. Through his dealings, he knew a very small company, Toei Musen Co., Ltd. based in Tokyo that specialized in assembling TV receivers, TV monitors, and TV kits for hobbyists under OEM brands. Mr. Yokota's network and personal involvement swiftly paid dividends. In less than 4 weeks, I was asked to move, by September 20th, to *Kansai Kenshu Center* (Kansai Training Center), Suitashi, the city famous for hosting Japan's Expo 70.

Phase one was immersion into five weeks intensive Japanese language and cultural training. There were forty trainees from Korea, Taiwan, Thailand, Malaysia, Peru, Indonesia, Brazil and India. We learnt the language formally and in the moments of fun. We had festivals of different countries with foods, dances and dresses. We developed strong bonds of friendship, which have survived the test of time. Even today, some of us remain in contact. Towards the end of the training, we went to the south of Japan; Hiroshima, Beppu, and Kita-Kyushu for a Japan experience. The visit to Hiroshima was the most traumatic experience of my life; Japan being the only country to experience the atomic bomb. The museum and hospitals where survivors were treated even today speak loudly of the ghastly memories. Therefore, the Japanese sensitivity against nuclear proliferation is quite intense and naturally understandable.

As noted earlier, Japan from day one was something very difficult for me to explain. I felt as though I were home. My four years of efforts and 1,000+ letters apparently had won the hearts of many people. Mr. Komai's secretary, I came to know later, read every letter of mine with appreciation as had many others. The lack of response, I recognized after having lived here, did not automatically mean that these letters were thrown in wastepaper basket. Apparently I had created a good impression on the recipients for my beliefs, values and perseverance. When meeting face to face, their affection was so obvious and they tried everything to make me feel comfortable. For six months every weekend I was spending either lunch or dinner or even home stay with one of the recipients of my communication. It was a pampering of highest order.

Lesson

Create Trust. It takes time.

CHAPTER 10

NO SURPRISE, PLEASE !

The future belongs to those who believe in the beauty of their dreams...

Eleanor Roosevelt

In October I moved to Tokyo. *Asia Bunka Kaikan* (Asia Culture Dorm) was my home for next two years. Like Kansai Kenshu Center, ABK housed trainees and students from diverse countries, pre-dominantly from East Asia and India. Upon moving to Tokyo I joined Toei Musen. It was a small, compact outfit of 50 people spread through a three-floor building. Their primary products were black and white and color television receivers and monitors. Mr. H. Nakajima, the President, greeted me warmly.

Initially, I was assigned to PCB (Printed Circuit Board) assembly. The work was soldering the various components (resistors, capacitors, and transistors) onto pre-designed circuit boards. These boards were then moved on to other working stations such as yolk mounting and final assembly testing. My first opportunity of assembling a color television set came in February 1970. It was a milestone worth recalling. The plant manager, Udagawa-san, insisted that I must focus on the objective for which

I joined Toei Musen. It took me almost 2 weeks to put all pieces together and once it was ready to switch on, I was nervous. Mr. Hara, my supervisor, having watched over my shoulder during the entire process, encouraged me to switch on the TV with assurance that there should be no problem because I had just followed the mechanical route. In spite of his encouragement, I politely requested him to take the lead and he gladly did so. Hara-san moved swiftly - connected the cord into an AC outlet and switched on my TV. Lo and behold ... it was working! "Wow", I thought. It was one of the finest moments because I moved one step closer to actualizing my vision. The whole team came to congratulate me. In order to commemorate this historic occasion for me, I invited them to dinner at a nearby Indian restaurant, Ajanta. It was their very first exposure to spicy Indian cuisine and most of them liked it.

I started taking Japanese language lessons twice a week in the evenings. In addition, I joined the Television Engineering College in order to learn the basic fundamentals. However, I was forced to drop out after a few weeks because everything was in Japanese language.

During those days, the Indian students and Trainees Association was very active in promoting Indian culture in the Japanese community. The Indian Embassy was, as they have always been, highly supportive of our cause. Within one month of my arrival, I was made secretary of the association. We had a lot of fun. We had no money but plenty of time. I remember when Sonal Mansingh, the famous Indian dancer, was performing at Expo 70 in Osaka. Before her return to India, she wanted to perform in Tokyo. I was on phone for almost 40 hours requesting everyone's cooperation. Mr. Saiichiro Misumi, Managing Director, Indo-Japanese Association arranged the Tojo Kaikan Hall and within 72 hours, we had a standing-room-only audience of more than 700 people enjoying her spectacular performance.

It became apparent to me that within one year's time frame, attaining the working knowledge of Japanese language, television receivers manufacturing and its basic fundamentals (all being in Japanese language) would be a daunting, if not impossible, task. Meanwhile, my promise back home was to return to India after one year. Renu was waiting for me. Mummiji was pressing me to get married. I started to consider my options. Of course returning home to get married and coming back to Japan was the most ideal situation. Another option was to request Renu to come to Japan and to be married here. Her grandparents had visited Japan to see Expo 70 and so had some experience. Therefore, I approached them with my idea as a sounding board. Instantly they blessed the idea and they become ardent supporters in persuading everyone back home. However, Papaji did not like my idea. His desire was to see Renu wedded with his own eyes. It was understandable from his perspective as Renu was the eldest of his daughters.

At this time I was also on the screening committee for candidates applying for Association for Overseas Training Scholarship' (AOTS). Through this selection process, I came across many applicants from Asian countries and became friendly with many executives of host companies. I started picturing in my mind a career for Renu – although I had not yet shared this idea with her. I was so swept away in my fantasy that I took for granted that she would love to excel in a career of fashion designing. I was enamored by its glamour. I never considered that she may not like it or what kind of dream she might have for her life after she became Mrs. Deven Arora. I was only thinking to give her as a gift on her 22nd birthday on October 9, 1970. I wanted it to be something unique, something memorable, something surprising. Therefore, while I was working feverishly on this project I kept it as my own secret.

One of the key learnings in my life has been that no one likes surprises ... whether bad or even good. My former boss and mentor, John Trani, had this written on his wall ' No Surprises, Please!'. Whether in business or life, this is so true.

Lesson

No one likes surprises ... whether bad or even good.

CHAPTER II

THE TOUCH OF MIDAS

Hope sees the Invisible, feels the Intangible and achieves the Impossible.

For the next three months, I worked with AOTS and Kanebo Christian Dior very closely answering their many questions. Why should an Indian girl learn fashion designing? What kind of linkage exists between the saree and western style dresses? What is her background? How much does she know about fashion, ladies dresses? On and on it went. Mr. Chiyoda, the final decision maker, kept on saying 'No'. He believed that my real intention was to use fashion designing as a ploy to get Renu to Japan at Kanebo Christian Dior's expense. He firmly believed that it would be hard for a traditional Indian girl to become a fashion leader simply by going through this training. Chiyoda-san kept reminding me that I should not make her life in Japan miserable. He was also concerned that, should Renu enter this program, her work should not be perceived as an act of 'forced labor' which was then a prevalent sensitivity. In retrospect, Chiyoda-san was absolutely correct. His observations were so accurate. We went through all the scenarios he described so painfully later in our lives.

Mr. Hideo Nakajima, my Godfather, was very close to the top management of Kanebo Christian Dior. He always came to my rescue and this time was no different. I shared my desire about Renu. He asked me only one straight question: Whether it was my plan or her dream. In my excitement of getting Renu to Japan, I responded that she was my fiancée. Our parents wanted us to marry and live together as soon as possible. Therefore, she also wanted to come to Japan. If I told her all the details she would not be able to make an accurate mental picture, as she had never been to Japan or anywhere else outside India. Therefore, she would certainly leave the decision to me by saying 'what you do would be in our best interest and that even if I did not like I would do my best to adjust and gradually transition to what I want to do'. Mr. Nakajima seemed to understand me, but I believe in his heart he did not agree. In communication, *understanding* and *agreement* are two critical but different components. If people would focus on these two I believe that most of our issues would go away including the conflicts of bigger scale. We do not have to agree on every issue but the understanding where the other person is coming from wins half the battle.

Mr. Nakajima virtually 'forced' the decision on Mr. Kozaburo Kitada, Managing Director, Kanebo Christian Dior. Mr. Kitada, on my request, spoke to Mr. Chiyoda. Renu's application went through formal AOTS approval cycle and on October 9th, on her 22nd birthday, it was approved.

I wanted to call her immediately with the good news but I could not, due to a lack of money. I had to be content by sending a cable on the following lines ... "Accepted as a trainee for fashion designing at Kanebo Christian Dior. A memorable gift on your 22nd birthday. Congratulations!" My feeling was that everyone back home would be elated to the extent of bordering with envy but Papaji was still dead opposed about sending Renu to Japan without a marriage ceremony being first performed in India.

Her family friends, Mamta and Asha worked with Mummiji to change Papaji's mind. It appeared that he was fighting a lone battle because everyone thought that Renu had an opportunity to build a career in one of the top fashion design companies on earth. Mummiji and Pitaji consulted Panditji for an auspicious day for Renu's departure to the East. They requested Papaji and Mummiji to consider Renu spending one evening with them in my hometown, Meerut. They wanted to give her a grand send-off. They had invited almost 500 people. With all the pressure on Papaji he had to give in. Everyone around him was perplexed as to why he was dragging his heels. On the contrary, he should have been happy that Renu was going to Japan not only for getting married but for a career too. In his defense, he had some strong convictions and beliefs, which might have tempered his vision, but later in our life he would be Renu's staunch supporter and our leader.

Lesson

In communication, understanding and agreement are two critical but different components. If people would focus on these two, I believe that most of our issues would go away including the conflicts of bigger scale. We do not have to agree on every issue but the understanding where the other person is coming from wins half the battle.

CHAPTER 12

INDIAN COUPLE ON JAPANESE TV

Nothing is impossible to a willing heart...
John Heywood

On November 19th, 1970, Renu landed at Haneda International Airport, Tokyo. It was raining very heavily. One of Renu's precious gifts is that all the important events of our life are celebrated on rainy days. Her nickname is *'Ame Onna'* (A woman of the rain). We met after 15 months. It was a very long period, indeed. Everybody said that my face was the happiest that evening. Of course it had to be. She was beautifully clad in a red saree - a very sweet bride! I was the luckiest person.

During lunchtime at Toei Musen, I used to watch a very popular television program known as *'Aoshima Yukio no Wide Show'*... the great show of Yukio Aoshima. It was hosted by three top stars of that era: Yukio Aoshima, Chinatsu Nakayama and Eita Yashiro. These three later turned into national politicians and Mr. Aoshima later was elected as the Mayor of Tokyo. The highlight of this show was performing marriage ceremonies with couples that had interesting episodes to share. I asked Renu to watch.

Although she did not understand much of the Japanese content she apparently liked its uniqueness. With her encouragement I contacted Nippon TV, the station that broadcasted Aoshima's show. I was told to speak to its director, Hideo Kurita. He listened to our story but was not impressed. Our story, he said, lacked the 'punch' that Japanese audiences wanted. However, he was kind enough to tell us to see him again after two days. At our next meeting there were four more persons, a panel of 5 including Mr. Eita Yashiro - one of the three hosts. Mr. Yashiro asked us a direct question in English; "What qualifies you to be on this show?" We had done our homework this time. We told them,

"You must have seen many foreign girls marrying Japanese men in traditional Japanese style. You must also have seen many Japanese girls marrying foreign men in traditional Japanese style. However, we do not believe that you have ever seen an Indian girl marrying an Indian man in traditional Japanese style."

That was the clincher. Mr. Yashiro proclaimed, "You are a very thoughtful and lovely couple. It'd be our honor to have you on our show". January 14th, 1971 was the last edition of this marriage special, therefore, we were told to be ready. However, there was a schedule conflict as we already had marriage plans for January 15th at Hirakata-shi. It was a 'pickle'. They kept on discussing for more than an hour. They had a problem dismissing us as Mr. Yashiro had already said 'okay'. However, to add one more edition was even more difficult as the programs were planned three months in advance. Mr. Kurita was in a difficult spot. After a few phone calls and more discussion among themselves, he said with a deep breath that he would find a way to do it on January 21st. His face was red with mixed emotions - happy for us but with a big headache as to how he could shuffle the program.

'Indian Couple on TV', so read the caption in Mainichi Daily News, a major daily English newspaper on January 22nd.

NTV Studio, Yomiuri Hall in Yurakucho, Tokyo, has a seating capacity of about 100 persons. I thought of inviting His Excellency and Mrs. Vincent Coelho, the Ambassador of India. Ambassador Coelho accepted our invitation saying not only that they would bless us on TV but that he and Mrs. Coelho would also grace the party thereafter.

January is Japan's coldest month and it was raining again heavily on the 21st. Despite the weather and against all the odds, virtually the entire embassy staff arrived for the televised wedding. Many friends – recipients of the 1000-plus letters which I had written from India but whom I had not had the opportunity to meet, also attended. Our company's staff, Kanebo, Toei and ABK teams joined. It was a full capacity attendance.

During the one-hour show, Renu was advised not to speak a single word except the phrase '*Zen Zen Wakarimasen*', meaning 'I do not understand at all'. The three TV personalities asked several questions including "Who is the guy sitting next to you?" This drew tremendous laughter when she answered "*Zen Zen Wakarimasen*". His Excellency Mr. Coelho commented that the marriage by the two Indian nationals in Japanese traditional style is not only a memorable event but it brought India closer to Japanese hearts as well. Culturally, both nations share similar values and this marriage would hopefully lead many Japanese to try to get married in Indian style. It was an experience to remember forever.

Later in the afternoon, we had a reception party hosted by Nippon TV. Most of the friends and well-wishers came directly from the studio. Dr. C.B.J. Rao, an esteemed senior colleague from ABK, was the master of the ceremony. Mr. Hideo Nakajima did the simultaneous interpretation in english for the benefit of the Ambassador, Mrs. Coelho and Renu. Mrs. Coelho presented Renu a return ticket for two to Sapporo, Hokkaido, for our honeymoon. Renu had never seen snow before.

We sent a creative 'Wedding Information' card to all our well-wishers around the globe. It had our picture in a Kimono and a clip from Mainichi Daily News. It was very well received. Papaji kept on asking for more and more to send to his friends. Renu became a celebrity appearing in Asahi Evening News and many weekly magazines.

Lesson

No problem can stand the assault of sustained thinking.

■

CHAPTER 13

KIKI (CRISIS) - WITH HARDSHIPS COME CREATIVITY

In the middle of difficulty lies opportunity...
Albert Einstein

In the first week of January 1972, a colleague of mine, Dr. C.B.J. Rao told me that Far East Procurement Operation, GE Audio Systems was looking for bi-lingual project engineers. I called immediately and one Bill Lawrence came on the line. He asked me to come over that afternoon. From the very first second of my entrance in his office, I sensed a click. Bill initiated with me in Japanese but he could not sustain the conversation. He laughed with full lungs. After fifteen minutes in the interview, he made me an offer, Yen 95,000 per month. I became bold ... "could I get Yen 120,000." Bill said that if my performance were per his expectation, within one year he would exceed my asking price. With a very little negotiation, we agreed on Yen 100,000. He asked me to join from the next day. Nothing in our life has gone that simply. I learnt that "If it seems too easy then it probably is."

Now I had a big issue with the Japanese Immigration Law. I had come to Japan on a trainee visa for 6 months duration. This visa was extendable for 3 years maximum. Now I wanted to change to a working visa and the immigration officials opposed this change. Their argument was that I had come to Japan as a trainee on a government scholarship whose primary objective was to transfer the technology in my chosen discipline for the betterment of my country. I had signed a contract promising that I would return to India upon completion of my training. Now it appeared that Government of Japan had invited a citizen of India, trained him at their cost to take away the job opportunity that otherwise a Japanese national was entitled to. It was a "No, No!" They recommended that I return home. I requested to the Immigration Officer that he give me a chance to speak. He promised to listen patiently. I said I agreed with him 100%. However, the reality was that with all education in Japanese, it was so difficult that I had not even accomplished 30% of my objectives. With all the battles of 4 years in India seeking permission to come to Japan I just could not go back empty-handed. I just could not do it. I needed his help in finding a solution to my problem. He sympathized immensely but his decision would not change. I started visiting the Immigration Bureau everyday at 9:00 a.m., whether rain, snow or sunshine, to explain my side of the story. The officials admired my persistence but their verdict remained unchanged.

Meanwhile, Bill Lawrence at GE was getting impatient. He told me that the job could not be kept open forever and that I needed to give him a date. Based on my input he would make a decision whether or not he could afford to wait. I had no date. I told him very honestly everything that had transpired and what I was doing to rectify the situation. He had no clue as to why it was so difficult for me to come to work. He was my admirer and knew the background as to how I came to Japan. He asked my level of confidence in obtaining a work permit. With all humility, I requested him to keep the job open for a few weeks and I would bet my life on it. Bill said, 'Okay, this job had your name on it.

Tell me how GE and I can help you to get official permission to work on my team.'

This blank cheque had emboldened me to look beyond the Immigration Bureau. Directly from Bill's office I visited the Ministry of Foreign Affairs (MOFA). As luck would have it, I came across a gentleman, Mr. Susumu Shimaoka at MOFA help desk. He is the most unlikely Japanese I have ever encountered in thirty-five years of my stay in Japan. A graduate of Tokyo University (the most prestigious institution in Japan) he is a very simple, jovial, down-to-earth and family loving person. He had an extensive network in almost every field and was a contrarian thinker. His philosophy was opposite to prevailing wisdom believing in the simple ambition-free, carefree mode of life. Most of the days, he would be home around 6:00 p.m. He did not drink and of course abstained from the traditional salary-man nightlife. He did not take more than five minutes in understanding my issue. He recommended hiring a lawyer and preparing a list of documents. Once these were ready, I was to visit him again.

I happened to know Koichi Inasawa, an attorney of repute since ABK days. He had been helping foreign as well local students through many different activities. He was widely traveled and well connected through Rotarian activities. He was a very influential personality and had an excellent network within government circles. On my request, he spoke with Bill Lawrence asking for GE's letter of guarantee, return fare of my family to India if something unfortunate happened to me, minimum salary of Yen 150,000, and a managerial title to prevent me being perceived as 'cheap labor'. Bill listened very patiently. He replied that GE was a global company with many rules and policies. While he would very much like me to work in GE it did not, however, mean that he could agree to all Inasawa-san's requests. He did emphasize that the Government of Japan values GE and, therefore, Deven would not be regarded as cheap labor. Bill did not agree to increase my salary and could not provide a managerial title. He said these are not given in GE, Deven had to earn through his toil. The other documents he agreed to provide. Later on, I learnt that he had his own internal battle. His Japanese staff had questioned as to why an Indian national was getting preferential treatment. In their logic, if I were American or Japanese it could be understood but an Indian national looked like a square peg in a round hole.

With all the documents approved by Inasawa-san, I delivered them to Shimaoka-san. He asked me to make 5 sets. Since my visa status was to be changed from 'Trainee' to 'Working', Shmaoka-san told me that I had to go out of the country and reapply. The nearest place would be to go to Seoul, Korea. He gave me the contacts of the key people in Japanese Embassy there and he also called them personally and sent one set of documents in advance so that it would be a quick turn-around. Inasawa-san then took me to his friend, Mr. Kato, a director at Ministry of Justice, in-charge of immigration matters. After reviewing all of the documents and GE's guarantee he commented that everything should be all right. However, I had hit one snag ... I did not have money to go to Seoul.

Renu suggested that I explore with Bill creative possibilities to finance the trip.

Bill had been monitoring the entire saga - the flurry of preparations. With great trepidation I asked him whether he could send me on a business trip to Seoul. He didn't quite understand the question. How could he send a person not yet on board to Seoul on GE's behalf? Crazy! But he also understood the reality.

After consulting with Human Resource and Finance functions, he told me, "You rascal, you are not coming cheap to GE. I'm putting my neck on line just to get you on board. You would better deliver! I will chop off your knuckles otherwise." He said the plan was that a Japanese engineer needed to visit a supplier in Seoul. Since he did not speak english I needed to help him in his communication. GE would pay me a fixed amount for my services. It would cover me for 5 days. In case it turned out to be longer, then I was be on my own.

Shimaoka-san had already done the advance preparations and Renu was talking to him on daily basis. She was carrying a set of documents all the time. Shimaoka-san called Renu on the third day informing her that the visa had been granted. All I had to do is go to Embassy of Japan in Seoul. Renu called me at Seoul to give me the happy news. It was the first overseas call in her lifetime. After 8 weeks of sweat and blood, I finally joined GE on March 6th, 1972.

Lesson

Adversity reveals genius, prosperity conceals it.

CHAPTER 14

FOLLOW THE LEADERS

Unless you try to do something beyond what you have already mastered, you will never grow...

Ralph Waldo Emerson

In the very first week of my life in GE, we had a serious design issue on the motor of a tape recorder we were buying from a leading consumer electronics manufacturer. This created a quality issue on the units we had already purchased. The quantity involved exceeded one million units. My primary job was to communicate the issues, provide probable solutions and implementation plans among the various functions of suppliers and marketing, engineering in our headquarters located in Syracuse, NY and our own team located in Tokyo. Bill was leading the charge. I spent over 80 hours in the office and supplier's plants. After the dust settled, Bill said, "Deven, welcome to GE." I became a trusted ally to Bill. He took excellent care of me. He was a workaholic and drove me very hard. It was fun. However, in late 1973 Bill decided to go back to the US to start his own venture.

During the same time I came across two other remarkable GE leaders who continued to influence my life for the next two decades. They provided me necessary 'pull' and exposure to ensure that the management in the US recognized my potential. The first was John V. Kese. He was my mentor from day one. He was a charismatic, warm-hearted, avid communicator. He always listened and respected every one's perspective. Everybody liked him. He had great talents, amongst which was his own homespun collection of quotations for every occasion. He taught me that 'reward of good work is always bigger challenges'. It is so true. He also taught me to eschew the phase 'I sent the letter!' It was a bureaucratic expression meaning 'My responsibility is over as soon as the letter is off my desk. Whether or not anything gets done is not my problem; it becomes the responsibility of the notified party'. Realistically it never happens that way. In big companies bureaucracy can breed its own culture. John always took upon himself to challenge such idiosyncrasies. He never accepted any BS (bull shit) and never passed the buck.

The second was Tomoji Okada. He was an industrial designer by profession but he knew every aspect of the procurement operation. Tom, as he was known, was a US educated Japanese national. He brought perspectives from both sides of the Pacific ocean. Americans always paid attention to him because his balanced views were in the best interest of business and therefore GE. He was disciplined and demanding to himself and expected the same from those around him. He never - never - gave up. Whatever he undertook, he saw it through. He was my boss for a few years and always kept me on my toes. He used to tell me that I was not pushing myself hard enough and that I could do better.

With our roots deeply anchored in the land of The Rising Sun, Renu prospering in her cooking career, and Adi in the safe hands of kindergarten, life was becoming a mechanical routine for me. Having been with GE for eight years I felt that I had reached a dead-end. The Far East Procurement Operation, Audio, was a fairly small shop. As I had become so good in my daily chores it took only 50% effort to deliver 120% output. I was on autopilot. Bored, I started doing some side business helping Japanese companies buy products and services from India. It was an instant success. I was paid 2% commission from the invoice value after the shipments arrived in Japan. My business was growing and I was prospering. Taken by success, my focus was naturally shifting towards this side business and the distraction started taking a toll on my performance on GE projects. To handle my private business I would take Friday or Monday off, two or three times a month. Tom Okada noted this change in my behavior. First he was concerned about the deterioration in my performance but then, after learning the cause, became very angry and accused me of 'being irresponsible'. He summoned me in his office one Tuesday morning - as on Monday I had taken sick leave.

It was a closed-door session for four hours. His charge was that I was a lethargic person, taking leave on the pretense of illness. It was impacting my track record and I could be denied future promotions if I did not restore my prior performance. Having said that, however, he did add that he had seen no issue with my output. In fact, people in Syracuse, NY had not even noticed slackening in my work. Tom's point, though, was that if I continued down this road there would be a point of no return, which, according to him, was very close. I was livid. I asked, 'If my output is okay then what is the issue? I am delivering the results with integrity. From my perspective, I am not motivated because I do not see any change in structure and do not know what you think about my next assignment.' If I could choose I wanted to be promoted to Tom's job managing the entire operation. However, because of the seniority system, American ethics 'Japanized', there were at least three persons ahead of me by virtue of their being in the company longer. Those colleagues had no chance until Tom moved and I had no chance until they moved. I felt stuck. Tom replied, "You are not ready for this responsibility." My thinking was that I could do better than many seniors because I brought a global perspective and in certain cases could even beat Tom himself like in networking and communication. The only thing I lacked was that I had not been allowed to visit the headquarters in Syracuse, NY - and on what I perceived to be the flimsy grounds of no budget even though most of the other team members went twice a year.

Tom listened to my frustrations very patiently. He was taking notes. At one point I told him that I wanted to quit GE and the only reason for my hanging around was that GE guaranteed my visa. I gave him many examples of my successes:

- My Toastmasters Presidency, where I cultivated contacts, managed the club, increased the membership and improved the club profitability.
- My side business, where I had developed important and useful channels with business people in Japan who depended on me in making their business profitable by getting, with my help, quality products from India on time.
- My track record of eleven years in Japan. I was clearly a survivor.

I told him that Tokyo management had not adequately recognized my contribution to GE's success. Therefore, working here was not fun. Tom was stunned with my level of desperation and unhappiness.

He invited me to dinner the same evening. He knew my weakness. Some people eat for living but I live for eating. The place was Hama Steak House in Roppongi. He ordered a nice Kobe beef steak and a bottle of red wine. During dinner he spoke on many subjects that had nothing to do with my career or me. Then gradually he switched over to me. He outlined the course of action: He would send me to GE Management Development Institute,

Crotonville, NY for a course in 'Development of Purchasing Skills'. GE Management Development Institute is also known as GE University. Courses offered are of the highest quality. The faculty comprises of professors from leading universities as well as GE's senior management. Therefore, it is the best of both worlds, a balance of theory as well practical insights. The course would sharpen my negotiation skills and enhance my knowledge of purchasing contracts and strategic supplier development. It would be a big plus to my career. On return, he would let me spend one week in Syracuse, NY. It was almost a three weeks trip, and also, he would promote me with immediate effect to Assistant Manager, thus making me fourth in line to take his job. My salary was to be increased by 11%, a hefty increase.

Then came two lessons of my lifetime. First on health: He said that keeping in excellent health is a lifetime project. Whether I am sick or not depends on my attitude. According to him, our brain is our computer - whatever signals we feed into this computer we would get a corresponding output. "If, on getting up in the morning, you think, 'Today I'm sick' then you are feeding to your brain computer that 'I'm sick', therefore, the net result would be that you will become a sick person. You are what you think you are. Every morning when you see your face in the mirror you must remind yourself that 'I am responsible to keep myself in the best shape for the whole of today.' It is going to be the best day of your life." His thesis was that in 99% of the cases even if I am not in the pink of health I would fight being sick by taking preventive measures such as a proper diet, avoiding excess alcoholic beverages, taking an adequate dose of vitamins, keeping a daily exercise regimen and following whatever medications were necessary to keep me fit. My computer would keep me alert. My whole attitude towards health would be different, positive and I would do everything to stay positive. His message was that if I wanted to become president of a company or a country or whatever,

I must first manage my own body; therefore, the very first step towards taking bigger responsibilities is to manage my own health. It was so revealing yet so simple. I had difficulty in believing it but I promised to follow his guidance beginning from that moment. I committed to him that I would never fall sick again. Since then twenty-five years have passed and I have not taken another sick day. The same is true with Renu. Adi set an example in St. Joseph, earning a medal of honor in four-year perfect attendance. Since then, my whole attitude towards health is different. I am very conscious of my body and if I feel that I am about to fall sick from fever, cold, etc., I take immediate precautions. I keep on reminding myself that I am in optimum shape. The effect is amazing, Norman Vincent Peale's 'Power of Positive Thinking', indeed.

The second lesson of the evening was the secret to climb on the ladder of success in any institution: I was told three letters to remember, P, I, E.

P was for '**Performance**'. It is the critical step. It must be better than the best although performance alone would not guarantee promotion. He agreed that my performance was very good: 8-plus on a scale of 10. He also knew that whosoever had come in my contact would be confident to get his things done and that he would be kept posted on its progress. He commented that I had the drive, enthusiasm, leadership, creativity and above all perseverance. However, these traits alone would not get me his job.

I is for '**Image**'. This is equally critical. 'Your image is your brand. Manage it'. What kind of image am I projecting on my peers, customers, suppliers, seniors, and managers? Every one counts. Unfortunately, my image was not of a matured person. He gave me a few examples. I was emotional. While emotions reflect passion you must balance emotions with logical thinking, situational analysis, and complement these with recommendations. According to him, whenever any complex issue hits my desk, I only communicated with the people concerned. It simply made me a 'cheerleader'. The recipient of the problem also expected me to communicate possible solutions and my recommendations, as I was closest to the action. (S.K. Patil also gave me the same golden rule twelve years prior to this – I would have done well to remember his teaching). Therefore, every issue or problem had to be accompanied by my recommendation and analysis as to how I arrived at this conclusion. Until I excelled in the art of solving complex issues logically, management would not be persuaded to promote me to the senior job.

E was for **'Exposure'**. The greatest impact on your career for both internal and external opportunities. You must be visible to those who can influence your career.

This is the privilege granted by the boss to provide exposure to more senior management. It is like making the presentation to the top management or outside organizations on his behalf. Therefore, the boss should have enough confidence in me that I would not damage his reputation or the image of the organization. On Tom's scale of 10 for maturity and PIE, I was just 5. He promised to work with me to increase myself to a 9. He challenged me to stand to his test in six months.

The final factor was my dress. I did not reflect professionalism, according to Tom. In 1980 Japan, executives did not wear flashy clothes. Their dress code was simple navy blue or gray suits, white shirts, and brown/blue neckties with black shoes. It looked like the whole of Japan worked for IBM. I always enjoyed wearing very different kind of clothes. Tom strongly disapproved my leather jacket, bold striped blazers, pink shirts and red color ties. My love for color did not conform well to Japanese norms.

F 6

Tom used to tell me that Jack Welch would fire me on the spot if he ever saw me wearing a pink shirt. That was a great day of learning.

My respect for Tom Okada had always been very high. He was very strict with me but behind this mask was his expectation to see me grow. He continued to monitor my progress until 1993. He was truly a GE leader trusted by Jack Welch, John Trani, Chuck Pieper, Goran Malm and Tim Murai, the GE top management team. I personally believe that he gave his life for GE. He was afflicted by cancer of stomach.

GE Yokogawa Medical Systems was in deep crisis in 1991 and Tom was handed the responsibility to change the image of its Sales Division while continuing to grow sales. His family, wife Kako, son Takuya and daughter Sanae were highly opposed to that assignment. However, he told his family, "My days are numbered. Why not let me die in doing what I enjoy the most?" He virtually worked until the last days from his bed at Keio University Hospital, Tokyo. He was 57.

Lesson

1. *You are what you think you are. Every morning when you see your face in the mirror you must remind yourself that 'I am responsible to keep myself in the best shape for the whole of today.' It is going to be the best day of my life.*

2. *The secret to climb on the ladder of success in any institution is to remember P, I, E.*

   *P was for '**Performance**'. It is the critical step. It must be better than the best, although performance alone would not guarantee promotion.*

I is for **'Image'**. This is equally critical. 'Your image is your brand. Manage it'. What kind of image am I projecting on my peers, customers, suppliers, seniors, and managers? Every one counts.

E is for **'Exposure'**. The greatest impact on your career for both internal and external opportunities. You must be visible to those who can influence your career.

■

CHAPTER 15

OWNING OUR PROPERTIES

The starting point of all achievement is desire. Keep this constantly in mind. Weak desires bring weak results, just as a small amount of fire makes a small amount of heat...
Napoleon Hill

Mr. Toshio Tanaka, founder of famous *Delhi Curry Restaurants*, was a trusted and loyal fatherly figure for us since ABK days. Tanaka-san was an entrepreneur with four restaurants. He was very fond of Adi. He used to visit our apartment often. During one of our conversations, he suggested to Renu that paying monthly rent to a landlord does not get anything in return. However, if we could own a small apartment then the same monthly rent (plus alpha) could be converted into building equity. Looking to the future, it might turn out to be a wise investment. We never thought that we would ever be able to own a property in Japan where land was more costly than gold. It was a struggle just to make ends meet. We both made a mental note for an appropriate time in the future.

In January 1977, I thought of giving a present to Renu on Adi's 2nd birthday. I remembered Mr. Tanaka's suggestion.

Although I had little faith and confidence in its outcome, I thought there is nothing to lose in trying. Renu and myself did not have the so called 'Hamlet Disease'. Between 'should we do' and 'shouldn't we do', we always thrived on doing. If we failed there would be a lesson learnt which would help us in our future trials. With this concept in mind, I visited Mitsui Bank head office in Hibiya Park. I had a saving bank account there since I joined GE in March 1972.

At the housing loan counter, Mr. Yasutake greeted me. He, to my surprise, was a very unusual banker - quick in making decisions. He was equally fast in speaking and did not mince words. He would do whatever he said and, if he could not, he would say so right away and on your face. While I was exploring the possibility, he was busy taking down notes. He made it crystal clear to me in the beginning of our session that Mitsui Bank had not granted even a single housing loan to any non-Japanese. However, having said this, he added that it did not mean that they would never do so. It would be judged on the merit of its case. If I was credit worthy and could clear the bank's criteria, I might be the first *gaijin* (foreigner) to secure a housing loan.

Having lived in Tokyo for almost seven years, I noted that Japan was opening up to outsiders. In my case, immigration, Dr. Kohda who gave birth to our son, Aditya... his first ever foreign child in 17-year career, and now the housing loan - clearing all the obstacles gave me a feeling of being a pioneer. It was an exciting time when Japan was in the formative stage, putting its systems and processes in place for *gaijin*. For the next 30 minutes, Mr. Yasutake questioned me and answered my queries. His simple and easy-to-understand replies encouraged me. One or two questions of mine needed complicated answers. He lost his temper. He kept on reminding me he was a very busy man. He pointed me to many prospective customers waiting in a queue to get their turn.

Mr. Yasutake's objective was to get done with me quickly. Thereafter, I answered his questions with no interruption. At the end, he summarized everything concisely with the parting comment that he would need seven working days to reply. Since I was a foreigner and they had no precedent yet, my case had to be approved by the senior management of the bank. I could not resist asking the last question, what his assessment was on my case. He was absolutely non-committal but added some facts for me to draw the conclusion from: That I worked for GE and GE was Mitsui Bank's number one foreign customer. That I had my saving bank account in their headquarters since the past four years. That I had never defaulted on payments.

I told Toshio Tanaka-san my experience in Mitsui Bank with Mr. Yasutake. He laughed. Based on what he heard from me he felt that even Yasutake-san could not say 'No' immediately on my face. He had to put up a kind of show so that I did not feel segregated as the *gaijin*. 'Seven days later' was an excuse to say 'No'. His advice was that I should not bank high hopes on its outcome. We both had a hearty laugh and I said "Let's forget about it."

After seven working days, as he promised, Yasutake-san called at my office. Our group secretary, Honjo-san, told him that I was on a business trip to Seoul, Korea. She would ask me to return his call when I returned. For my job I called the Tokyo office daily. Honjo-san told me about Yasutake-san's call. On my enquiry about any message left by him, Honjo-san responded laughingly - neither did she inquire nor did he volunteer. Since she felt it was a rejection call, it would be better for me to learn from him directly. On return to Tokyo, I went to see Mr. Yasutake. He was busy and asked me to wait. As soon as he was free he called me to his desk. In a very friendly tone, he enquired where I had been. He had been looking for me for almost a week. Then he focused on the subject. The message given to me was that the management of Mitsui Bank would consider my application just like they do for an average Japanese citizen seeking a housing loan, which meant that I had cleared the first *gaijin* hurdle. If I could prove that with 10% of my monthly salary I could pay the installment continuously they would consider approving my loan. He structured a 25-year loan repayment plan with 5.6% interest. Based on my gross annual income then I was entitled for Yen 6 million maximum. Mr. Yasutake guided me to look for a condominium in 7 to 8 million Yen range. He gave me another advice saying that he did not know how much savings I had but that the down payment should not exceed 3 million Yen. "Therefore, before applying for housing loan, go and look for an apartment in this price range." He wished me good luck. The reality was that we had no funds. I was not prepared for this outcome. It was a very big and serious commitment. I just wanted to forget the whole idea.

A few Sundays later, Tanaka-san came to our apartment. Since he was involved in the restaurant business he needed to import ingredients, accessories and many other items from India. Since my ABK days he had sought my help in communicating with Indian suppliers, writing letters, translating their responses into Japanese, and whenever he met some Indian, he always asked me to help him. He offered me remuneration for my services but I thought 'I am not a professional, it is not my job', so I told him I would continue *gratis* as a friendly gesture. He being like a fatherly figure, I asked him to please continue to take care of my family. Tanaka-san was very nice to us. Renu and I were his trusted allies. He always used to cite our examples to his staff and many other friends for our survival instincts. He asked me the result of my follow up discussion with Yasutake-san and profusely congratulated me for moving up on the ladder one rung. I told him candidly (anyway he knew it already) about my finances and made it known that I was not interested in pursuing the housing loan further. He listened to me quietly with not a single word spoken.

With Renu and Adi away in India, in 1976 I joined Tokyo Toastmasters Club. Dr. Ralph Smedley in Orange County, California initiated the Toastmaster movement. His vision was to empower people to achieve their full potential and realize their dreams. In a friendly environment of a club, its members anywhere in the world can improve their communication and leadership skills, gaining the courage to change. His key message was that people learn the most while helping each other in moments of fun. With this objective in mind, through its member clubs, Toastmaster International was helping men and women, over half a century, learn the arts of speaking, listening and thinking – vital skills that promote self-actualization, enhance leadership potential, foster human understanding, and contribute to the betterment of mankind. We met every Thursday evening for two hours. Our club had about 30 members. It was fun to be with them. I was so much involved that within one year I was voted to be the President. I would spend so many hours improving and enlarging club's activities that Renu became worried. She asked John and Tom to bring me down to reality that my employer was GE not Toastmasters - 'Therefore, be loyal to your paymaster.' Toastmasters gave me an opportunity to find my true self: My strengths and weaknesses. During my Presidency, I was fortunate to have made acquaintance with the leaders in diverse field, Michio Nagai, Minister of Education, Yoshizo Ikeda, President, Mitsui & Co., Ltd., Nobuhiko Ushiba, Japan's ambassador to the US, Takamiyama Daigoro, the very first foreigner to have entered in *sumo* world – Japan's traditional sport of 400 years of history, and many others. Takamiyama's speech had special significance on a *gaijin* like me. He observed that being a bi-lingual person is very difficult. He narrated his experience ... if he was talking to a Japanese person he felt that he could explain himself better in english language and if, on the other hand, he was communicating with a native english speaker he felt he could do a better job of explaining with Japanese language. His conclusion was that he was not good in either language. I was on TV, newspapers and many magazines to promote the Toastmasters movement that was devoted to making effective oral communication a worldwide reality. It was great fun.

At Toastmasters I became very friendly with Mr. Fumiaki Okuno. He had lived with his family in India for many years as the manager of Mitsui, India. Okuno-san was equally active in Toastmasters. Of course, his communication skills were of par excellence. His beautiful and spacious house was very close to our apartment. Since I was alone I used to frequent his home. We had dinner together every Thursday after Toastmasters meeting.

One Saturday morning, Tanaka-san invited me to have lunch with him. He loved owning beautiful cars. He had bought a new one and took me for a ride. It was Jaguar .... My God, the first experience in my life. During lunch, he touched on Yasutake-san's green signal to go for a condominium. He said he had looked up some condominiums on my behalf and they seemed to be reasonable, having a good secure location and were close to the station. I was not very enthusiastic but went along. We continued for many weekends. We might have seen more than 100 in a period of seven weeks. Some were very good but exceeded the budgetary limit given by Yasutake-san. Some were too far from the station or commuting time exceeded two hours each way. While I was going through this ritual, I sensed that Tanaka-san had something on his mind. A common friend of ours introduced us to Mr. Sugi. He was a TV producer. His wife was of Polish heritage but born and brought up in Kobe. Sugi-san was looking for a buyer for his apartment since their two children were growing fast and he had already built another. His problem was that Mrs. Sugi had modified that apartment for the taste of foreigners, which did not appeal to Japanese. As soon as I entered it I was in love. The apartment was so beautiful, located on the 11th floor with a great view. It was a part of the newly developed community with approximately 200 condominiums and facilities like outdoor swimming pool, car parking, and a private gym. I was delighted to see this but I knew I would not be able to afford it. Still, Tanaka-san recommended that I go for it. From there until we went to the bank where Tanaka-san took the lead. He negotiated the price from 11 million Yen down to 9 million Yen. Sugi-san could not say 'No' to Tanaka-san. Tanaka-san hosted a great dinner for Sugi and his family in his Ginza restaurant that evening. They are still very good friend of ours until today.

It was around 11:30 p.m. when Tanaka-san took me to a quiet bar. He knew that I was not happy because I did not have any funds. Here came the greatest compliment of my life. He told me that he had yet to see a family like ours, so dedicated to each other, loving and compassionate. With Adi we had more responsibilities. It would be his honor to be worthy of doing something for us. He then offered that all the expenses above the bank loan of 6 million Yen would be paid by him as a token of his friendship. We did not even have to worry about its repayment. I was fairly drunk at that time but still retained my senses. I do not remember exactly how sincerely I expressed my gratitude, but one thing I remember telling him was that we were talking about my two years salary and getting a free ride would not be acceptable. He then counter proposed that it could be a loan without interest on an as-and-when-I-could-afford-to-repay basis. I had no choice because I did not know how things would unfold anyway. The following week, I requested Tanaka-san to accompany me to meet with Yasutake-san. Yasutake-san moved swiftly. When he saw Tanaka-san with me, he said Mitsui Bank had nothing to worry about. He knew who to talk to if I did not pay my monthly installment on time. Here was the last hook - they needed a co-signer on the contract. Tanaka-san told me that he could do. Yasutake-san asked me whether I knew someone in Mitsui Group who might agree. His rationale was that it would speed up the process if someone were coming from within the same group. As my case was unique he did not want it to be dragged down.

I had dinner on Thursday night as usual with Okuno-san after a Toastmasters meeting and explored the possibility. He simply asked me where he had to sign. He said, "Recognizing good people does not take years. It is the first few seconds that defines whether or not you have the chemistry." During his stay in India, his family was accorded so much love, friendship and trust by the Indians, so it would be his privilege to be of value to us.

I needed 3.0 million Yen but Tanaka-san loaned me 3.4 million. It seemed like too much but, then, I knew nothing about buying a property in Japan and was unaware of the many complications I was about to learn. At every stage I would have to cough up money. He was so accurate. I insisted on signing a contract for his loan. He said that writing a note on plain paper, acknowledging the receipt of funds would suffice the purpose. In early April, Sugi-san gave me the keys.

It went so fast that that I did not even write a note to Renu in India. She was undergoing intensive cooking training inside the main kitchen of Oberoi Sheraton, Bombay under Chef Richard Graham. She had no clue as to what I had been doing in Japan. Partially, it was that she was living a life of an owl, working in the nights and sleeping during days. After every thing was finalized, I asked her to return to Tokyo by the last week of April so that we could move to our new home. She did not believe me. She thought I was joking. How could we own a property when we did not have enough funds to survive day-to-day life?

My biggest concern was whether she would second my choice. This was the decision, a major one of our life. But she was very happy. We owe to the two persons immensely: Yasutake-san (we became life long friends) and Tanaka-san (without him, dreams would not have become a reality). These two gentlemen would continue to play significant roles in our lives for many years.

On May 10th, 1977, Adi, Renu and myself moved to our 'own home' in Yokohama. What a feeling it was.

From September Renu started teaching Indian Home Cooking to Japanese housewives. It was an instant success.

In 1981, Renu's cooking classes faced two issues; coping with a decreasing number of new student enrollment and retaining the existing students for a longer period of time. The reason for the decrease of new students was that the area around our home had been 'saturated'. In four years, Renu had already reached 1,500 students. We spoke to many people in Tokyo area asking them to join the school knowing that they had a genuine interest to learn about spice usage and authentic India cuisine. However, the biggest impediment was the location of the classroom. It took 60 minutes or more each way from the center of Tokyo to visit our house in Yokohama. Additionally, we were not tapping the cash-rich office working ladies segment because they could come only in the evenings and their journey to our location was not an attractive proposition. Secondly we needed a wider repertoire to retain the existing 1500 students. Suggestions made to us included expanding the choice of courses to Chinese, French and Italian dishes. Renu believed that Indian cooking's history and varieties are already so diverse that in her entire life span neither could she learn nor could she authoritatively teach it all. Therefore, she would stick to Indian cooking and expand her own knowledge. Currently 16 courses are on offer as compared to only one in 1981.

Mr. Toshio Tanaka suggested that before moving to Tokyo it would be wise to gauge the reaction on a pilot scale. For this purpose, he offered his daughter, Urala's mansion (condominium) as she had moved to live in with her parents. It was located in one of the most sought after locations in Tokyo, Yushima. We planned to offer classes twice a week, Tuesday and Thursday, and we made the announcement in the newspapers.

The classes were a huge success. Evening classes, which she did for office working women, or 'OLs' (office ladies), were very crowded. It was her first time to run evening classes and it was a successful experiment proving that there was a tremendous interest. With these successes, we saw a clear signal to move to Tokyo. We started looking for houses and condominiums. I suggested Renu to take lead because she had to look from the angle of teaching cooking. We made the rounds of viewings on almost every Sunday. After six months of search, in October 1981 we came across a mezzanine flat with a spiral steel ladder connecting the two floors. On the first floor, it had a large living room, kitchen and dining room. On the mezzanine were two bedrooms. It was perfect for cooking classes. It had been built one year before but had not sold as yet because Japanese were not used to that kind of living and for *gaijins*, it was small and expensive. We fell in love with it at first sight. As soon as Renu entered the 'mansion' (condominium), with only one foot inside, she said with tremendous excitement, 'That is it! Let's go for it! I have made my decision!' Adi and I were surprised with such an instant outpour of emotions from Renu. Apparently, she had found her dream house. Her eyes were gleaming at the sight of the spiral steel ladder. The more she saw inside, the more she liked it. It also had a security lock to protect from unwanted visitors. Its location was in the most prestigious area of Tokyo, Takanawa, very close to Gotanda station of Japan Rail and two subway lines. Of course, it was very quiet with 'who's who' living in the neighborhood. I asked Aditya, six years old then, what he thought about the property. He seconded his Mom's selection.

We asked hesitatingly its price. Yen 80 million - nine times more than what we paid in 1977 for the Yokohama condominium. My first reaction was 'We can't afford this'. Renu, like a sitting bull, was resolute, and then declared that she needs this house only and that she would discontinue all further searches. It was a challenge of monumental proportion.

Renu and I approached our generous benefactor, Yasutake-san of Mitsui Bank. He told us that with a maximum stretch we could get Yen 60 million, based on our combined income. Compared to the time of the 6 million yen loan in 1977, our 'net worth' had increased ten fold. I was amazed to see our own progress. He candidly told us that he could not support this purchase as, according to his observation, we did not qualify for it. However, Renu was determined to find a solution. Our options were first to negotiate the price down by contacting the landlord, Kawase-san, directly, and to find a seed money, Yen 20 million, from other sources for the down payment. The landlord, Mr. Toru Kawase, was a gem of a person. His mother owned the old property. It had been demolished to build a three-floor building that housed four flats for sale. The Kawase family occupied the third floor and three flats had already been sold. The fourth, which interested us, had been difficult to sell due to its unique design. Approaching Mr. Kawase saved him (as well as us) the commission to be paid to the real-estate agent. We introduced ourselves. He and his family liked us very much. Renu told them that it was a dream house. He asked Adi's opinion. Adi responded in his lovely style, '*Boku mo suki desu*' (I do like it too). We told him honestly what Mr. Yasutake of Mitsui Bank told us. "We want to buy it but we can not afford to pay more than Yen 60 million." We requested him to consider our offer. He was gracious and told us that he would also like to sell it to a family like ours. He reduced the price down to Yen 75 million but could not go further. We requested Mr. Toshio Tanaka to have a look at the 'mansion'. He also liked the property. During the meeting with Kawase-san, Tanaka-san told him about his 12-year association with us. He told the entire story as to how we bought our first property in Yokohama four years before and requested the rock bottom price. Kawase-san consulted with his wife and mother. His mother liked Aditya very much. After fifteen minutes, Mr. Kawase told Tanaka-san that his last price, leave-it-or-take-it, would be Yen 70 million. We were very excited that we were narrowing the gap but we were still Yen 10 million apart - a big sum. We decided to continue the talk with Kawase-san. He still had no other candidate buyer. He was paying interest to the bank every month and we thought knowing of our continued interest in his property might some day persuade him to lean in our favor. It was a wishful thinking with prayer. We were hanging on with our teeth and nails.

Kawase-san had two hobbies, drinking and smoking, and he excelled at both. Several times I was invited to drinking sessions at his home. He was home after work around 6:00 p.m. From 7:00 p.m. through midnight he would drink and smoke heavily. Although I did not smoke at all and drank only lightly, I enjoyed his company due to his very warm-hearted nature. We did not talk about the price of the mansion. He was keen to hear the stories of what we were doing and how we survived in Japan. During one of the sessions I found him very happy. Later in the evening after a fair dose of liquor he told me that he had found a buyer of the mansion who was willing to pay Yen 75 million. He would sign the contract the following week. He felt sorry that he did not have the privilege of our neighborhood but sincerely requested to stay in touch. The news brought Renu to a state of shock. She wanted Kawase-san to deliver the property to us on his offer of 70 million Yen. We thought of suggesting Kawase-san to accept 60 million Yen. The balance (10 million Yen) we would pay in monthly installments and we consulted Tanaka-san regarding it. We were already paying him, on a monthly basis, for the loan of 3.4 million Yen, which he had provided, us for buying Yokohama property in 1977. His felt that it would be a big stretch for us. His rationale was that monthly payments to the bank, Kawase-san, if he accepted, and for the other property would exceed 33% of our combined earnings, destabilizing our life for which we worked so hard. His recommendation was to look for another property that we could afford. But we had already put in almost ten months of efforts. Going for a new search was not an appealing proposition. I decided to meet Kawase-san with the fervent hope that his deal with the other buyer did not materialize. It was good that I contacted him.

His deal with the new buyer had fallen through but he did not feel like telling us. Kawase-san was hoping that we would still be looking for a property. He knew in his heart that Renu would not settle for any other property and that we would contact him again. I became bold in our negotiation and told him that we had been talking for almost one year - that demonstrates our sincere desire in his property. He had been paying interest for over two years to the bank, which I guessed has exceeded 10 million Yen already and if he sold us the property, he would be relieved of this pressure, that 60 million Yen was the best price he could fetch from us, and therefore, he should sign the contract with us on the very day.

Initially, he said 'No', but a few drinks later he asked for a couple of weeks to think. Meanwhile he read an article on Renu in *Bungei Shunjuh* written by Mr. Doi Masaharu, Japan's leading gourmet critic. Bungei Shunjuh is one of the most prestigious monthly magazines of Japan with very high quality articles, significantly influencing the intellectual readers, like academia, business executives, and professionals. Therefore, it has a loyal readership from all walks of life. In the magazine Doi-sensei lauded Renu's efforts in bringing authentic India cuisines to Japan by teaching the spiritual, medicinal and fine taste of spices to Japanese housewives. Having read this article, Kawase-san was so excited that he said it would be his honor to have a family like us in his building and he agreed to sell the apartment for 60 million Yen. We took occupancy in October 1982 after twelve months of negotiation with Kawase-san.

This success story made headline in my office in Japan and the US. My negotiation skills were admired to the extent that I was called upon to negotiate the most complex deals in Korea, Taiwan, China, Hong Kong and, of course, in Japan as well. The other side of the coin was on many occasions at work I could not deliver the targeted outcome for various reasons. When this happened I was admonished that I had not achieved the company goal because I had not put my heart into the negotiation as I had for buying my own property.

In 1989 Renu's business was expanding and there was no privacy in the existing home. We thought of buying one more flat nearby. Once again the search started. We found two candidates quickly. One was in the same building; our neighbor James Yoshida's, priced Yen 200 million, and the other 8 minutes away, priced 150 million Yen. Mr. Yasutake, our good benefactor at Mitsui Bank since 1976, came to our rescue once again. He looked at Renu and myself with a smile and said we are eligible for either one, based on our track record and net worth. I told him that in the preceding thirteen years of dealing with him he had never been so generous. I just could not imagine that in 1976 in getting the Yen 6 million loan and in getting another 60 million Yen loan in 1982. They were a struggle. But in 1989 we could think of 200 million Yen without a blink. He told us that we knew the answer in our heart. With little debate we settled with the one at 150 million Yen because living in the same building was not much different from living in a maisonnette apartment - just an extension. Stress plus work would easily be transported to the new home. However, if we are 8 minutes apart there is a possibility that Renu would not keep going back to work in the midnights. We still believe it was the right decision. We moved to the new house on June 17th, 1989.

There are some distilled lessons I learnt in this process, which I thought to share here:

1. *Raise your level of aspiration. Even though the challenge may be formidable, believe that it can be achieved.*
2. *Communicate candidly about your limitations and flexibilities.*
3. *Invest time. If it is important, let the other party feel it.*
4. *Build trust. Honesty and sincerity pays big dividends.*
5. *Hang on in there with teeth and nails.*

■

CHAPTER 16

FROM 'DOER' TO 'LEADER'

Success... seems to be connected with action. Successful men keep moving. They make mistakes, but they don't quit...
Conrad Hilton

Year 1982 was the landmark year of our life. We got our Japan Permanent Residency Permit (equivalent of 'Green Card' status in the US) on February 23, 1982. It is a status equivalent of being a Japanese citizen with all the privileges and obligations. The only exceptions were that we did not have the voting right and could not contest for a political office. Our benefactors, Susumu Shimaoka-san and Koichi Inasawa–san, graciously guided us in its entire undertaking. It was the smoothest ride of our visa journey in thirteen years of our stay.

It was the year in which Renu started her 'Gourmet Trip to India'. Many of her students, having heard of India, its culture and mystique, from her for so long, had started pressing her to plan a short trip to India with them. Since 1982, until today, she has done almost fifteen trips of this series.

While we had a busy home front, GE Audio business was going through a major upheaval. Jack Welch, CEO, made it known that the businesses which did not have a long-term strategic value, technological innovation and sustained profitability, those he called 'Three Circles', were candidates for being fixed, closed or sold off. Although GE Audio was a $400 million business with handsome profitability returns, it could not be a stand-alone entity. The audio business had provided one unique value to GE management, serving as a training ground for budding high potential executives. Indeed, each and every general manager of audio business, who successfully managed, was elevated to Corporate Vice President. Paul Van Orden, Walt Williams and John Trani were the shining examples. Still, we unknowingly faced a five-year strategy to divest audio/consumer electronics. We had no privy to such sensitive information. As John Kese used to say, slaves are sold and not fired.

The first phase came when GE Audio was combined with the video (television) business. It was then renamed GE Consumer Electronics. Total sales became $1.2 billion-plus. This change was very positive for my career. It was the beginning of an era where I continued to grow for the next 17 years in GE. This reaffirmed my faith that change is positive, bringing growth and creating new opportunities. I was promoted to Manager, Audio Products, a $100 million portfolio, which was very profitable (with delivered very high productivity). Our motto then was 'shed blood first before you accept even a cent increase.' With the promotion I had (new) power, recognition and new responsibilities. The team in Syracuse had tremendous confidence and trust in my sourcing capabilities and supplier management skills. I was their 'Prince' and they protected me from all the internal battles. I was told just to focus on 'getting the job done'; tell them what I needed, and they would find a way to deliver. I was given a four person team. Our charter was to reduce price by 8 to 10% every year, maintain the highest quality and deliver on-time weekly shipments based on what we committed to or agreed upon. In doing so, air shipments were never an option because of the associated exorbitant costs.

During my ascent to bigger roles, William G. Smith, Vice President for marketing, became interested in me. Bill was a soft spoken, very jovial and down-to-earth leader. It happened that in 1984 Chicago Consumer Electronics Show, I requested him to give me an opportunity to have a breakfast meeting. These shows were very busy and executives like Bill had to take care of customers, distributors and big accounts. My feeling was that he would say 'No' not because he did not want to meet me, but because his time had a premium. To my surprise, he said 'Okay for 7:30 a.m. next morning'. It was the second day of the show, which was supposed to be the busiest day from a business standpoint. Due to jetlag and a missed wake-up call, I got up at 8:00 a.m. I rushed like hell and with US$10 in tips to hotel doorman to give me preference over a long queue for taxi. I managed to be in the restaurant around 8:45 a.m. I was certain that Bill would not be there and, even if he were there, that he would be mad as hell - to the extent that he would never see me again. To my surprise, he was there waiting for me. With a smile he said, "Welcome to the US." Then he added, "Now you understand the feeling that when we come to Asia we want to miss late dinners." I was tongue-tied. During that meeting I explored whether I could call for his guidance on complex business related issues. I just wanted him to give me his perspective. He was three layers above me in the company hierarchy. He said 'Okay', and advised me to call him at home around 8:00 p.m. his time. He was very disciplined, to the point and did not provide direct answers to my questions. He used to play a devil's advocate role. He always took the opposite view of the solution I proposed. He asked, "Why are you doing like this?" "Why did not you think of this?", etc. In such brainstorming sessions I used to find my own answers. He was, therefore, in a true sense, an excellent mentor.

Bill's godfather in GE was Paul Van Orden, Sector Executive, Corporate Executive Committee (Paul rose through ranks starting from GE Audio, Syracuse, NY), and Bill was mine. It appeared there was an informal line between Paul – Bill – Deven. I noticed that people were careful when they talked with me about organizational issues. Yet, on the contrary, if they wanted any message to go higher-up, they talked to me in such a way that it become my issue and I would be motivated to approach Bill. I was very careful and just kept on my level. Bill, as far as I knew, rarely spoke on my behalf. His objective was to support the Asia team because that was where all products were coming from. He had a unique career including a stint as a journalist in the Vietnam war. He used to paraphrase H.L. Mencken's famous quote, 'One thing we learn from the history is that we learn nothing from the history' - countries and organizations alike keep repeating the same mistakes over and over in the name of progress. He taught me to capture the big picture, build the team, have confidence in myself and enjoy. He was always there to help me until 1987 when he moved to a new position outside GE.

Our first test came with the Yen's very strong swing. We had limited options. We had to move out to countries where Yen had least influence. Taiwan and Korea were the closest. We transferred roughly US$60 million worth of products to Korean companies like Samsung, Gold Star, Daewoo and Insung. With this transfer came the issues of delivery, quantity and, of course, quality. My whole team spent more time in Korea and Taiwan. We were stretched. I recall in one year alone, 1984, I made over forty trips to Korea ... Seoul, Inchon and Suwon. It made me very famous in Seoul. If a supplier in Korea needed to know my schedule, all he had to do was to call Seoul Hilton Hotel and he would know the schedule of my next three trips. At Kimpo Airport, Seoul, customs officials recognized and remembered my face. One of the reasons was that all the mock-ups, samples, drawings, etc. that we hand-carried, were shown as samples of 'no commercial value'. Officials always questioned us and we were asked to pay duty. It was my job to persuade them that these samples were brought in to generate more business for their country. Higher custom officials recognized that GE was creating more job opportunities for Korea and our samples were released without any duty payments. As other colleagues could not do that kind of talk, I was called upon to get samples cleared through Korean customs. As a result, custom officers also became friendly.

We had to explore other untouched pastures like China. In 1982, I made my first trip to Beijing. It was then a very primitive place. Its airport was very dark. Beggars were around right on the airport. As soon as we came out we noted oxen carts were plying stuff. It was a cultural shock like going back to the 18th century. We had confirmed reservation at the newly opened Shangri-La Hotel. When we arrived at the reception we were told, "Sorry, the government has blocked two floors. Therefore, no rooms are available." When we asked for alternative accommodation, their response was that they did not know what to do and they could not be of much help either. We were six persons in total, three from the US and three from Japan. I was so upset that I demanded to see the owner or the President of the hotel. My concern was that my three colleagues from the US had just traveled sixteen hours. We needed to provide them a roof to shelter under. After almost an hour of arguing, shouting and fighting, they found three rooms. They suggested that we manage by sharing these rooms. In Chinese culture that would have been okay, but not in the US. Anyway, I said that our American friends should take possession of those rooms and we would continue to talk. I again requested the manager to give us three more rooms. The response was 'No way'. I shouted at the top of my lungs. A government official, apparently unrelated to the hotel, approached me and asked in broken english how he could be of some help. He took me to a separate room and asked what was the problem. I showed him our confirmation slips. He did not understand my language but the message went across that we needed three rooms. He took me to various levels in the hotel and negotiated on our behalf for two hours but with no success. At every rejection, my mercury was going higher. He did however, secure three rooms for us from the next day, but nothing was available for the first night. I demanded that we be given one suite for the three of us, and we offered that we would pay $1,000 for that night. However, all the suites were booked too. Meanwhile, our 'friend' (government official) was busy calling many places. It was 12:00 midnight. We were dead tired. This friend came to me and said that he had persuaded another official to open a guesthouse for us for one night - free of charge. Not only did the hotel arrange the car but we were also provided three beds in the end. When we arrived at the so-called 'guesthouse', it was in fact a warehouse, very dirty, no sanitation and no water supply. Finally at 2:00 a.m. we tried to sleep but we could not. It was such a situation that we could not even go to toilet. We returned to the Shangri-La at 6:00 a.m. and stayed in its lobby. At 7:00 a.m., to our utter surprise, we were given three rooms. We checked in and finally slept for three hours. Based on my 30-odd years of travel, the more you demand from service industries like airlines, hotels and restaurants, the better the service you get. 'They operate on the principle of The Squeaking Wheel Gets the Grease – FAST!'

Chinese businesses, especially the audio manufacturers we visited, were mostly state owned enterprises. They had the latest equipment but it was still inside the packing crates. Even those that were out of the box were not operational. Price fixing was an issue. No supplier could give an accurate quote. When we asked for back up details the answer was they would hit our target. During our one-week visit of Beijing, Shanghai and Shenzhen, we met or visited over twenty suppliers but we could not find anyone we could do business with. The China Business Association in Tokyo had introduced those suppliers. They apparently had high potential for export but we found nothing.

Our alternative was to work with Japan, Taiwan and Hong Kong-based suppliers who had production facilities in China. They too were going through enormous pain in terms of delivering quality products on time. Moving to China had not resulted in 30% price reductions as we hoped for. However, these initiatives were of strategic long-term value. In the ensuing years, our supplier base was 90% shifted away from Japan.

Our business selling audio, video and communications (telephones, citizen band receivers, CBs and walkie-talkies) was very price sensitive. We shipped more than 5 million units annually. Even a one-cent increase in price ... well, you can calculate the impact. Therefore, it was imperative to ensure no price increase in purchasing. In fact, our charter was to find a way to reduce cost by 8 to10% every year. There was a very famous saying in consumer electronics; every year units have more features, improved quality, better appearance, smaller size, better industrial design, smarter packaging and wages go up **but** the unit price will be lower. Take the history of Sony's Walkman. Every year, if you observed, the size became smaller, more features were added, the packaging became very colorful, wireless head phones produced better sound and comfort, and yet the price went down to less than half within five years of its introduction. This is the power of competition - fierce competition in fact.

With the supplier base moving away from Japan, the next challenge was to match the team around where the action was. We needed to reduce the number of employees in Japan and build the team in China, Hong Kong, Korea, Taiwan and the Philippines. This restructuring was very painful but would prove not to be the last such exercise in my career. Moreover, the Japan team had to eliminate their jobs while training their counterparts in those countries. While doing so the impact on GE's sales, profitability and market share must continue to be more positive every quarter. It meant no compromise on performance; scaling down the operation in Japan where expertise and experience resided while coaching the teams in Asia. The entire process was an experience that taught me many lessons.

One of the unique cultural lessons I learned was when we were hiring an electronics engineer in Manila for quality inspection job for telephones. Mike Yamada, Quality Assurance Manager, hired a local consultant to help us. Amazingly we received about 200 applications for one opening. The consultant told us that GE was one of the most admired employers in the Philippines so we had the opportunity to select the very best candidate. What surprised Mike was that from 200 applications about 140 were female engineers. Looking from Japanese cultural lens, Mike promptly eliminated those 140 female applicants on the grounds that this job would be tough for them to handle. He did not even see them. Out of the remaining 60, we selected the best candidate. He was of course a bright young man. Our local consultant, a Filipino, was watching us with great interest. After everything was over, he asked one question to Yamada-san and myself, "Why did not you even think of looking at 140 female applicants?" Mike's reply was that it was a demanding job. We believed it would be difficult for a female, even an engineer, to spend late evenings or weekends in suppliers plants. Suppliers would not hear her voice as she would be considered a 'light' person on the job. The consultant's reply opened our eyes. He intoned that he did not know much of hiring professionals practices in Japan but in the Philippines most of the banks vice presidents and other professionals were females. They had three or four children in average, and they not only reared their families but also balanced their private life with their professional career achieving outstanding results for their employers. His message was that since we had hired him as our local consultant it would have been effective to seek his advice on local culture and business practices. In today's globalization rush it is always tempting – but wrong to judge from our own culture, rearing and beliefs without taking the local values into consideration.

In 1986 GE bought RCA. It was at that time the biggest non-oil buy-out in corporate history. GE Consumer Electronics became an integral part of this new entity. Since RCA consumer business was $2.8 billion, the total size of our business grew to more than $4.0 billion. My job expanded and I became in charge of Personal Entertainment and Communication Products. The team size increased to 40 across Asia for a business of $150 million. My life became hectic and my role changed from 'doer' to 'leader'.

Within one year, GE made a further a bold and unique move, which became a classic case study in leading business schools around the globe. GE swapped its consumer electronics business with Thomson's medical business, CGR. By so doing, GE became global in the medical systems business whereas Thomson Consumer Electronics became a force to be reckoned with in global television arena. It was indeed a 'win-win' business strategy. As we were going through this turmoil, from GE Audio to GE Consumer Electronics to RCA Consumer Electronics to Thomson Consumer Electronics in around five years, the changes were very exhilarating for me personally. At every step of change I got promotion, more responsibilities, bigger teams to lead plus calls from other businesses. Change is an opportunity to grow. It is positive and exhilarating.

The day we became officially an integral part of Thomson Consumer Electronics, John Kese happened to be in Tokyo. He invited me for dinner at Hotel Okura. During dinner, Chuck Pieper, newly appointed President of Yokogawa Medical Systems (YMS) came to the same restaurant for dinner. John, of course, spoke reams of good things about me. Chuck offered me the job of Manager, Sourcing at YMS right away. It was a big operation, a big salary and a change from consumer to medical products – a new excitement. However, there was a clause in the GE and Thomson Consumer Electronics agreement that stated that GE executives were barred to return to GE for a period of five years. Chuck fought for me for two years. He tried to persuade my bosses at Thomson Consumer Electronics to allow me to rejoin GE but they dragged their heels. Finally, in 1989, Chuck spoke to John Trani, Chuck's boss and president of GE Medical Systems. John sought CEO Jack Welch's concurrence. Eventually the way was cleared for me to join YMS and I joined YMS on January 1st, 1990.

During my two years at Thomson Consumer Electronics, I learned the French style of management, which was absolutely different from what I learned for sixteen years at GE. It was political and dysfunctional. For example, my operational boss was located in Syracuse, NY, my administrative boss was in Indianapolis or Paris, and my Human Resources Director in Singapore. Three people controlled my job specifics, budget and manpower respectively. Due to distance, time difference and conflicting or misaligned priorities, they rarely talked to each other. However, the show had to go on. I made the decisions I judged appropriate for my organization and business. On my leaving Thomson in December 1989, I wrote a parting note to all the three bosses stating that my two years under them were very productive, and although they had not sharpened my managerial skills but they had made me a great politician. Thank you!

Lesson

Change is an opportunity to grow. It is positive and exhilarating.

∎

CHAPTER 17

WHERE MY SKILLS WERE CHALLENGED

The only limits are, as always, those of vision...
                                                       James Broughton

Effective January 1st, 1990, I joined Yokogawa Medical Systems (YMS). It was a joint venture between GE Medical Systems and Yokogawa Electric Co., Ltd. YMS was a large organization with over 1,000 people in all functions vertically integrated from buying, designing, manufacturing, marketing, selling and servicing supported by business development, human resources, legal, and finance. All these functions were housed in a newly built five-story building, other than sales and service, which were scattered all across the country.

The location of YMS was about ninety minutes away from my home, including an hour train ride. Normally commuting trains in Tokyo are jam-packed during morning hours from 7:00 a.m. to 9:00 a.m. In my case, though, I was spared of this ordeal as my journey was in the opposite direction of ordinary commuters. I could easily find a seat and could spend my time reading the newspaper and books.

There were many firsts in my joining YMS. It was the first time for me to work in such a large organization. It was the first executive role I took up at a Japanese corporation. Of course YMS was a nearly 100% owned GE subsidiary but other than a handful of American expatriates, the day–to-day business was run by Japanese people for the Japan market. Nearly all the founding management and staff had been seconded from Yokogawa Electric, a famous and successful Japanese public company, and they had brought with them the Yokogawa culture that had clearly overridden any GE culture. This was my first experience with the famous Japanese '*mikoshi*' management where no one person makes decisions, the group made decisions collectively. My immediate boss spent almost 95% of his time in meetings. His pet phrase used to be, "Let's meet again later because I don't want to be late for my next meeting." These were endless meetings with 60% of the participants sitting like mannequins. They would speak only if someone asked them a question or for an opinion. For the first time I worked in a sourcing operation whose most critical function was to feed the manufacturing lines, rather than a buying operation. The technology and engineering division would decide the supplier and dictate the prices. Manufacturing would determine the timing of delivery and quantity. It was also my first experience to spend three hours everyday in commuting to and from the office. It was the first workplace in my life where, in the first three months, I had no clue where to start.

Although I had lived in Japan for twenty-one years, it became apparent that I was living in a different Japan. YMS was the 'real Japan'. I began to feel scared that this job was a challenge beyond me. I had no knowledge of diagnostic imaging equipment like MRI, CT scanner, X-ray machines and Ultrasound scanners which used state-of-the-art technologies and which were highly complex and sophisticated life saving detecting devices.

YMS operated an intricate 'just in time' production system like the Toyota Production System (TPS) based on '*Kanban*'. Every supplier was given a schedule sheet specifying the quantity, date and time for refilling the *Kanban*. Their job was to drop the components into the bins reserved for them. Sourcing's function was to chase the suppliers for the quantity to enable the lines to keep running. Most of the buyers had bicycles, pedaling them to fetch the components. There were too many suppliers, most of whom had traditional links with YMS management. Suppliers treated the sourcing team just as delivery boys. Our customers were primarily hospitals and doctors about whom I had no knowledge and access. My 18 years of sourcing experience was primarily in buying relatively simple, portable, finished electronics products. My experience had no match with my new assignment. I had sleepless nights.

Renu recognized my state-of-affairs. She recommended that I see Chuck Pieper. One fine morning at 7:30 a.m. I went to his office and told him my inability to do an effective job, hence my wish to quit.

Chuck, in great astonishment, looked into my eyes. His face was red, and in full-throated voice he told, "Deven, I have been listening to heaps of praises about you for over two years. It looks like they were just baloney. I fought for you right up to Jack Welch. Now you have the guts to tell me that you want to quit. Go back and work on a blue print of making YMS sourcing the best global sourcing operation in entire GE, and deliver minimum 8% productivity every year consistently. You have all the qualities in making this happen. I will give you four weeks to come back with your plan."

Lesson

Faith delivers miracles.

CHAPTER 18

THE MAKINGS OF THE BEST GLOBAL SOURCING TEAM

*When you hire people who are smarter than you are,
you prove you are smarter than they are...*

R.H. Grant

Having been kicked like a soccer ball by Chuck, but heartened by his faith in me, I went back to the basics with which I started in 1965. The key mandates Chuck gave me were, first to build the best global sourcing team in entire GE and second to deliver 8% productivity every year. I embarked upon a plan for the next three months that would make me knowledgeable on my team - their strengths and developmental needs - the products and components we buy, and our strategic suppliers. This became my launching pad.

My title was Division Manager, YMS Sourcing. My team comprised of 40 persons. They were very courteous to me. Once, early on, I requested a buyer on my team to procure some information on a supplier. His response was, "Yes Sir, I will get back to you with your requested information very soon." Nothing happened thereafter. The same thing happened with another buyer.

She responded very politely to my request but never produced any information. That was my first experience in the Japanese culture of *honne* and *tatemae*. Of course I had heard a lot about this culture but I had never so openly experienced it and never at the job. '*Honne*' is what you would actually say, do or feel. '*Tatemae*', is a more logical answer or a view that you say or show to please the other. What those buyers were saying when they promised the information I requested was *tatemae*. In fact, they did not trust me enough to talk *honne*. The common notion was, "Since Deven doesn't understand our products, our suppliers, our customers or even Japanese culture he is not going to last in YMS more than six months. Why bother about a guy who won't be around long?" Even my boss, Satoshi Kurata, Managing Director, Manufacturing Division, used to tell me, "Deven, you just sit and read the newspaper. These boys would take care of everything." Mr. Kurata did learn later that in GE culture you had to anticipate change, adopt change and drive change, and while doing so, enjoy change. Probably I was his first lesson.

My observation was that Japanese people normally were very disciplined and hard working from 9 a.m. to 6 p.m., but thereafter it was a different story. In order to win their confidence, I needed to meet them in after office hours for dinner and drinking. I shortlisted 20 leaders whose voice carried weight and each evening I invited one person for dinner. The first invitee was Okano-san. He first said 'No' that he was very busy but I persuaded him anyway. He was very unhappy with me - I had taken his job. He was a veteran of over thirty years of experience. He had started his career with Yokogawa Electric and when YMS came into being he was one of 333 charter members, the founding fathers, of YMS. We went drinking. After he became tipsy, he started venting out his feelings. I just kept listening. Listening, unlike hearing, is a dynamic exercise. It involves three key functions: Watching the speaker's body language, analyzing the spoken content, and listening to the message itself. The toughest part of active listening process is to sustain concentration on the speaker. One thing that always worked for me was to take short notes. I continued taking notes in such a way that Okano-san did not feel offended. After about two hours of his venting, he revealed something I was not prepared for. He confessed that when I requested information from the buyers, they first sought his permission to go ahead. Okano-san was still calling the shots, and apparently he had decided to be non-cooperative. My only objective of the day was to listen and earn his trust. He was surprised that I kept cool. He felt I might become upset. I told him that my becoming his boss did not give me a right to command his trust; trust must be earned and it would be my continued endeavor. We kept on drinking past midnight. He was very relaxed. On parting, he said, "Arora-san, from now on I will cooperate with you because I like you." Japanese society, in general, becomes free of pressures during such sessions. Under the influence of liquor people are emboldened to the extent they could commit serious offense. Even if a guy committed a murder in such circumstances, court will take special note. It does not mean, however, he or she would go free. Therefore, *Sake* (Japanese wine) plays a crucial role in Japanese social life.

Within 3 months I had met all the twenty colleagues individually after office hours to determine *honne*. During the process I consumed tons of wine. It must be a record of a lifetime. Maybe it was focused or forced drinking. Renu always hates me when I return home drunk but it made me knowledgeable on my team's personal lives and their backgrounds, issues at work and their opinion on improvements, strengths, weaknesses, and dreams. One thing was crystal clear, that not a single person I met during those sessions had professional sourcing knowledge. They were primarily, as I guessed, delivery boys. They were doing what they were told without aspiration to become professional sourcing leaders. They did not even know what the buyer's job entailed.

Most of them came to sourcing because they were tired of sales, HR, finance or service and they were looking for a parking place to rest. Their general impression was that buying did not require any specific skill and that anybody could do the job. All they had to do was just beat on the suppliers to reduce the price or improve the delivery and quality.

I presented to Chuck my five step plan including revamping the organization with outside blood, acquiring mechanical or electrical engineers to talk intelligently with suppliers, bringing trainers from GE Management Development Institute, Crotonville, NY, creating a five year vision for YMS Sourcing, and initiating a global assignment program. Chuck smilingly responded, "Deven, you did not come cheap. I am paying you 15 million Yen a year. All the investment you are asking me to make with your plan - I need your commitment that in year 1991 you will get me 8% productivity (cost down)." I told him that he was fair and I would make that commitment. With the plan approved, came the toughest part, execution.

I started tapping within my old organization and other acquaintances and hired six persons within one year, Hideki Narita, Taiji Kimura, Noriaki Takei, Toshifumi Tsuji, Toshio Miyazawa and Norio Ishida. In addition, I requested Kurata-san, Yamaguchi-san, Managing Director for Engineering, Fujita-san, and Ryo Takahashi to provide me six engineers. It was the biggest paradigm change for them but they were cooperative during the entire process. It was, for them, a cultural change. At YMS, engineers were hired to design new products, to perform the 'brain' function. Engineers felt demoted by moving to sourcing, a support function. I spent hours and hours explaining that sourcing is a cash-generating engine for YMS. Every single dollar not spent on components and supplier services goes directly to the bottom line. The added benefit was that our products could compete more effectively in market place, resulting in more sales, which in turn produces satisfied customers, suppliers, and shareholders. Engineers, working with suppliers, could creatively reduce the price of the components significantly. "You will see the results of your actions quickly, and you will make YMS cash-rich." Yoshiyuki Ogawa, an out-of-the-box thinker, was the first engineer to understand my message and moved to sourcing. Thereafter, many others followed.

While this upheaval was going on, my team was getting scared. The label put on me was, "Deven wants to bring his own guys. He hates the YMS people." I did not worry, as my preoccupation was to get the job done. However, Tsuji, Narita, Kimura and others had to go through a very tough time. First, they were all Japanese. They received the onslaught of the fury. Second, survival in a Japanese business entity like YMS and adjustment to that culture was a bigger challenge for them than for me. I was spared because I was, after all, still a *gaijin*. We started seeing people finding sourcing as their home, including those who had not seen a long-range dream to become an integral part of sourcing. It was a very delicate process. We tried to make such transfers as smooth as possible, but for sure I was hated like hell. Many of the people did not talk to me for many years.

The next step was to train the team professionally. I proposed to have two professionals from GE Management Development Institute fly to Tokyo. Kurata-san told me there was no budget and, anyway, he did not believe that Japan had anything to learn from the US on purchasing skills development. I believed that there were certain fundamentals that were globally applicable. We needed to learn those and then modify them, based on Japanese culture. Moreover, we were developing a global team and they had to understand how to deal with American suppliers. With regard to the budgetary issue, I pointed out that management used it as an excuse for the things they did not want to do. "You always have money for the projects you set priority on. Correct?" I knew it was an expensive proposal to the tune of 3 million Yen (US$ 30,000) to fly two professionals for their task of one week but it was an investment to nurture the seeds for professionalism.

We took the entire team in January 1991 to YMS Kenshu Center (seminar house) on the foothills of Mt. Fuji. We also had two more seasoned professionals, one from Toshiba and Tom Okada who joined us. Tom accepted my request to provide my team a bigger perspective. He stressed on two themes: The buyer is the businessman who controls his company's funds, therefore, he needs to ensure whether he is getting the optimum value and that suppliers are businessmen using their resources effectively to enhance the speed. He noted that YMS had limited manpower and too many projects, and, therefore, if we depended solely on inside resources, our cost down efforts would be delayed. He suggested letting suppliers do the whole work and YMS people be the approvers - making the buyer the driver. We started creating news within YMS. Sourcing had had a reputation of being a backward and dark group. Driving the changes, we were becoming a model organization. Even Mr. Kurata started mentioning us with pride.

Tsuji-san was my most trusted lieutenant. Working with him was great fun. He was always there to take my pains and struggles away. We were known in YMS as one pair. If anyone wanted to convey anything to me, they always went to him first because it was easier to relate to him. He always told me to manage external politics and pressures whereas he would deal with internal issues. I'll bet his pressure was 100 times heavier than mine because, although being a Japanese, he was alien too in the YMS culture. He manouvered complex labyrinths with great care. He used to attend all those endless internal meetings until midnight. I asked my bosses to reduce my team's participation in such meetings. Yes, we did want to participate but as soon as our part was done we should be allowed to go. However, for Japanese group mentality, it was a very difficult proposition to accept. They were at ease only when they were in a group. As individuals they felt their identity was at risk.

The next step was to create a vision for my team. I worked with GE Medical Systems headquarters located in Milwaukee, Wisconsin and the person who helped me the most was John Christman, Manager of the Leadership Development Program. Together, we developed a 23 page document. It articulated what kind of dream an entry-level buyer could look for in the next five years. If one continued progressing, he could even become manager, sourcing. Tsuji-san, and my entire staff reviewed the plan and they adjusted the contents for YMS and Japanese culture. When we distributed it to the YMS management team, people did not believe that it could be possible in sourcing. Even marketing, sales, finance did not have such a concrete step-by-step approach in providing career growth opportunities. Most people did not even take the subject seriously. However, Tsuji-san was told me that there were many aspirants who wanted to join sourcing. We decided that we would be selective in offering slots. They had to meet our criteria. It was indeed a great feeling.

The fifth phase was to establish a global assignment program. In the global arena of GE Medical Systems, I worked with two esteemed colleagues, Bob Gouin, Manager, America, and Guy Moraux, Manager, Europe. John Trani used to call us 'The Three Musketeers'. We had global sourcing meetings every six months to share best practices and leverage of our buying dollars across the globe. During such sessions, I proposed to develop the global sourcing leaders by exposing them to different cultures, sending one buyer every year to Milwaukee physically with his family to work there as he was working in YMS, and vice versa. Once the program was approved, the Japanese spouses started clamoring that they did not want to go because of language, culture and fear for the unknown, the usual resistance to change. I told them they were making my life difficult by not availing such a fine opportunity GE was offering. I also told them to know that after one year they would see even a greater difficulty because they would not want to return. Most of the people had difficulty in appreciating what I meant. Every time I visited Milwaukee, I made sure that I called on the houses of those secondees. To my amazement, the wives told me they were enjoying life, having adjusted to the new cultural environment. They had made American friends and were enjoying weekend barbeques and golf. As I expected, their request was to extend their stay for another year. I had to say 'sorry' and they became disheartened. Our objective was to expose as many sourcing leaders as possible to the experience. Similarly, we had leaders from Milwaukee visiting YMS under this program. It started in 1992 and continued year after year. In 1993 Guy sent one leader, Eric Grislain, also from Paris. YMS sourcing became truly global. This initiative became a solid example of great learning.

Chuck left YMS to head GE Lighting, Europe in 1992 and we had his successor, Goran Malm who was even more enthusiastic about our initiatives. He encouraged our team to expand the focus toward across Asia. The first case was inviting Prapanch Mandana, Sourcing Manager, Wipro GE Medical Systems, India, to come to YMS for six months. He helped one of our key display monitor suppliers, Chuo Musen, to link with WGE's supplier in order to reduce their cost and to pave ways for a probable transfer of technology when economy ultrasound scanner production would be moved to India.

The second initiative was to strengthen GE Medical Systems, China sourcing. Tsuji-san and myself requested Tsuyoshi Matsumoto, Group Leader, Electrical Components, to consider moving to Beijing for a period of two years with his family. I asked him to make a decision within 24 hours. His challenge was twofold, to convince himself whether he saw this opportunity as a stepping-stone towards growth in his career and to persuade his wife and two beautiful children. I was proud that he did not disappoint me. I still believe that in the life of two children we made a great difference. China, where extensive opportunities lay in this century will always be closer to their heart. The images from their formative years must live vividly and, who knows, it might persuade them to go back to seek better prospects.

Next was Emiko Ishii. She was a dynamic person. We asked her to go to India. It was another first to send a Japanese female to India for a six-month assignment. Prapanch had to help her go through many cultural paradigm changes with his team in Wipro GE. The first one was Emi's acceptance as a professional buyer by his team and suppliers. In 1995 it was not a widely accepted practice to have a Japanese female professional interacting with Indian suppliers and negotiating deals but Prapanch accepted the challenge. Emi proved that she was at ease in dealing with global people regardless of country and culture.

The sourcing team, which I inherited in 1990, was truly global by 1995. I was amazed that it was possible. Chuck's charter was of course tough but doable.

Lesson

Real leaders are ordinary people with extraordinary determination.

CHAPTER 19

DELIVERING ON 8% PRODUCTIVITY COMMITMENT

There are four steps to accomplishment: Plan Purposefully. Prepare Prayerfully. Proceed Positively. Pursue Persistently...

Now that we had developed a team, it was time to remember that GE culture was numbers-based: 'We eat, breathe, sleep with and live by numbers'. Our sourcing team might have become the best global sourcing team in the entire GE but what good was it if we did not deliver 8% productivity (cost down) every year, the commitment I gave to Chuck in 1990? Based on my 18 years of audio experience, it was obvious to me that beating suppliers on costs were not going to yield $8 million every year. There had to be a unique, sustainable, win-win solution for our suppliers and YMS.

Jack Welch was very hot on 'workouts' then. Bob Gouin and Guy Moraux were already ahead of me in conducting 'Supplier Workouts' on a regular basis. Bob invited me to attend one of those in Milwaukee. I jumped on their bandwagon and sought their support. They were equally excited. However changing the paradigm back home was a tough nut to crack. YMS management would tell me that I was copying everything from the US without considering its feasibility in the Japanese environment. My intention was to share the best practices from everywhere as I thought we could always change or adjust them to fit our local environment. However, on supplier workouts, in addition to YMS management, our key suppliers and even my own team were divided. It was too big a change too soon and the 'fear for the unknown' always informs procrastination.

Supplier workout was a group session in which key stakeholders (participants) focused on a theme, issue or opportunity. A cross-functional team comprising of YMS functions and suppliers gathered to brainstorm creatively. As out-of-the-box thinkers, they considered *pros* and *cons* of their recommendations using process mapping and other tools available to them. This group then presented their recommendations with an action plan of 'who will do what and by when' to the management and other participants in a town hall meeting format. The supplier's representative made the presentation. Any participant could challenge their assumptions, recommendations or conclusions. As one cohesive team, the group had the responsibility to persuade the attendees to agree on their recommendation. The management team had three options:

- Accept the group's recommendation.
- Reject and send it back to the drawing board to redo.
- Accept it, but with modifications.

Once the management had bought it in, it became the commitment of the group. The management in turn empowered the group to execute their recommendations within three months and the management ensured that the group was provided with adequate resources including budget, if necessary. This group would continue to work together as one team and they would meet with the management after three months to report the outcome.

We faced three major hurdles. To begin with, creation of a cross-functional team within YMS was challenged by an excuse of 'No time'. It was especially coming from marketing, service and sales divisions. They saw no reason to deal with suppliers. "It's sourcing's job to reduce cost. They can and should do it." Yet, our rationale to invite those functions was to have a big picture. The so-called 'upstream' functions had the pulse of the market place. If the prices of our CT scanner or ultrasound scanner were reduced, it might boost sales against competition. Feature changes, on the other hand, might worsen our sales. Without knowing the market reality we would just be throwing darts in the dark. Second, within the sourcing team, confidence was lacking for driving the cross-functional team. Achieving a 30% cost reduction, on which I set my heart, was overshadowed. Third, the suppliers always believed that when their customers like YMS or GE initiated something new involving them it was another ploy to pull blood out of their already dried up veins. They smelled supplier workout as a trick to force them into another price down spiral. Thus, it looked to me as if it was mission impossible.

After a few sleepless nights, I took Tsuji-san out for dinner. Tsuji-san knew exactly what I was trying to do but he was very nervous. He suggested that I speak to the entire sourcing team so I called a meeting. Everyone was very doubtful of its success. The common line was that supplier workouts might be successful in American culture but in Japan it might fail. People working at various levels in different YMS functions were not happy in toeing to sourcing leadership. "Sourcing is firing YMS people and bringing people from outside instead. That's why the sourcing team is not getting their cooperation on day-to-day basis. If we introduced supplier workouts, our life would become even more miserable."

Another dimension was added, "Suppliers are shaky as they are perceived from the outside. Arora, Tsuji and Co. is making too many changes too fast".

I knew what they were talking about. I had told two of our key suppliers, Tokin Kogyo and Yokogawa Toa, that their prices were out of line and that they should find a way to reduce prices by 30%. One of the potential ways would be to move a part of their operations to China. By doing so they would not only help YMS but GE Medical Systems, China and they would make their other customers like Fanuc and NEC equally happy. The president of Yokogawa Toa was so mad that he complained to Mr. Sugiyama, YMS, Chairman, that Arora should not be allowed to visit his facilities again because I understood neither their business nor the prevailing relationship between the two Yokogawa-affiliated companies. However, both companies, with constant nudging from us under the relationship management by Ryo Takahashi and Tsuji-san, moved to Tianjin, near Beijing, in 1993. On completing ten years, Tokin Kogyo expanded their China plant. I believe Yukiko Matsuzaki, President and Yutaka Yamamoto, her #2, are visionary leaders.

The human brain is gifted to become more creative under tremendous pressures. I remember President Ronald Reagan's famous line: 'If you make your communication visual so that people not only see but feel the impact, then you can motivate them to act'. I tried it in my small and humble way.

On a white board I wrote the following:

YMS annual purchases	$100 million	
We need to save 8% in 1991 means	$8 million	
It means every quarter savings	$2 million	
It comes to per month savings	$700,000	(round-
It means per week savings average	$170,000	ing off)

With 5 day week, per day average $ 34,000
With 8 hours a day, per hour average $ 4,250
With 30 people in sourcing, per person average $140

It meant that every one of us had to save a minimum $140 every hour to hit or beat our commitment - and it had to be sustained every year. How should we accomplish this monumental task? I saw the faces in the room and my team was recoiling with 'Wow!' My message was, unless we adopted an out-of-box thinking this would become a kind of impossible dream. The sourcing team alone, howsoever brilliant and gifted it might be could not possibly succeed alone. We needed to expand our area of cooperation, bringing in more YMS functions, suppliers, global sourcing, etc. 'Make them the heroes. Our objective is to improve continuously the bottom line of YMS and GE'. The team started thinking on these lines. Tsuji-san, then, proposed a plan where every team member had to do the selling job of supplier workouts. In the following three months our efforts were frustrated because our explanations were not giving a visual picture. Nobody had a feel. We said, "We will take some risks. Just do it." Thus, we were finally set out to conduct our first YMS supplier workout in April 1991. I requested Bob Gouin to visit Japan in helping us launch it.

Five teams with eight persons (four from YMS - cross-functional, four suppliers and a sourcing leader) were formed with three simple messages:
- 30% savings on their own pre-selected project.
- One team.
- Develop a realistic plan, which is executable within 90 days with 'who does what by when'.

As to 30% cost reduction it could be material cost, process cost, design improvements, logistics, or anything that was found to be adding cost. They were encouraged to touch every possible area they could think of. There were no sacred cows.

As for making the group a 'One Team', all the eight persons were to be united to a team to challenge the project. No distinction between supplier or YMS functional divisions was permissible. They were to share all information freely unless it was absolutely company proprietary. The last mandate meant that they were to make every effort to win the management's buy-in. My sourcing division assumed the responsibility to keep the team focused on the task.

On a Thursday afternoon, almost fifty persons were aboard a coach going to YMS Training Center, the venue of our first Supplier Workout. Among them were suppliers, the YMS team, Bob, Tsuji and myself. Other than Bob and myself, no one had any workout experience. Almost everyone had the same thought - this is going to be a waste of three days including a Saturday holiday. I was worried I would probably be fired if this initiative did not bring the desired result.

Bob, with his skills and experience, adroitly took lead in kicking off the Supplier Workout. Day 1 was dedicated to 'Building the Team'. During dinner, five tables were set for the five teams. Still, they had lingering thoughts like why YMS marketing guys were drinking beer with suppliers. By the time the dinner was over and group exercises tackled together, all such thoughts evaporated. In fact some teams started talking about their projects right on the dinner table. Almost every team had a late night session with notes and computers; exchanging data while drinking beer.

On day 2, the five teams in their separate breakout rooms had the whole day to focus on their assignment. During the sessions, suppliers asked many candid questions to which they would have no privy to expect responses under GE's protection of classified information. One supplier engineer curiously questioned a YMS design engineer, "Why did you choose a 15 degree angle on this panel? Was it needed as a functional parameter?" Watanabe-san hesitated to respond for a minute because no one had questioned him about it before, but then answered candidly that it simply looked very attractive when he was designing it. This was typical of most of engineers designing products, sitting in their own cubicles, talking to almost no one other than computers. The engineer who asked the question said, "If you could reduce this angle to 10 degrees, the process of bending the steel plate would become easier and YMS could save as much as 10,000 Yen ($100) per piece." The seven members of his team looked at him and Watanabe-san found himself the center of attention. After a few seconds of thinking, he responded that he could live with 10 degrees.

Such creative juices were flowing in all the five rooms. Nobody was negotiating the prices. Ideas were being explored creatively and in an atmosphere of fun. Time and again, it has been proven true in my life that if the leader gives a clear direction to the team and then sets them free, the results delivered will be beyond the wildest imagination.

On day 3, Bob provided guidelines for the five teams to prepare their output to be presented to the senior management. Bob ensured that the presenter for every team would be a supplier's representative. His objective was not to force the supplier alone to live by the commitments. The real objective was that he or she who was making the presentation on behalf of the team would continue to execute, once the management had accepted their recommendation.

At 10:00 a.m. we had at YMS Training Center Kurata-san, Yamaguchi-san and Kawase-san plus many others from YMS along with the Presidents of the five suppliers. The hall was packed with almost 70 people. Bob introduced Team A. Mr. Shimizu, Managing Director, Tokin Kogyo, made the presentation. The output indicated a 30% to 35% total reduction. Most of the audience could not believe it was possible. After the presentation, there was a 10 minute question and answer session. Questions were asked, including those from the other four suppliers. All the eight persons from the presenting team answered logically. They had the back-up data to prove that the savings estimated were realistic. Bob then asked for the Managements vote. Not only did they accept the recommendation but they commended what they had seen: So much cohesion, team spirit, enthusiasm and determination to meet the commitment. Yamaguchi-san, YMS Director for Engineering and Technology, was always the first one to catch the wave of the future. He said, "It's wise to put your money where the results are visible in the next 90 days." He reaffirmed that the five engineers assigned on five teams would continue to work, and that there could not be a better opportunity. He became a very strong proponent of supplier workouts from that day and continued to help for many years. Another enthusiast was Mr. Shinichi Kawase who later in 1992 became the president of YMS. Mr. Kawase spoke very highly about our initiative in many journals including one for Japan Management Academy.

After all the five teams presentations were over, almost every one in the room was a convert. They had started feeling the impact of what Jack Welch was trying to accomplish at GE through workouts. I had a new lease on life, thanks to Bob, the sourcing team and, above all, the participants who made the commitments. Thereafter, it was easy to institutionalize supplier workouts in YMS.

Twice a year, in spring and autumn, for the next five years we conducted supplier workouts. We brought suppliers from the

US, China and India. Goran Malm encouraged us to do similar sessions in China and India. In January 1993, I was attending the GE Management Development Course in Crotonville, NY. During the occasion I invited Jack Welch to attend one of our supplier workout sessions. He, appearing truly flattered by my invitation, asked me smilingly whether he would need to drive to YMS headquarters in Hino. My response was, not necessarily, we would bring the session to him in central Tokyo. He was non-committal but he appreciated my request.

GE YMS had Quality Circles. Their primary objective was to do continuous '*Kaizen*' (improve quality step by step). Every function participated in them. Each year in February they selected the champion. In 1995, Kawase-san asked me to have a team from supplier workout compete. Tsuji-san and myself took the invitation as a challenge, and decided to go for 'gold', the championship. On February 23rd, 1996 among the six teams coming from entire GEYMS, our supplier workout team was voted the best, and Championship Cup was awarded to the supplier. The landmark, of course, was that the presentation was made not by a GEYMS employee but by an outsider. It was another 'First' in the history of GEYMS.

How did we do on our 8% commitment made to Chuck? To recap:

Year	Target (10%)	Actual (Billion Yen)
1991	1.4	1.55
1992	2.0	2.01
1993	2.3	2.30
1994	2.8	2.84 (11.36%)
1995	2.4	2.50

Goran commented: I realize the difficulty with measurements – but when limiting the results to sourcing cost down, your team's track record is great.

John Trani, President and CEO, GE Medical Systems, sent a congratulatory note to my team on December 9th, 1994. It read, "Congratulations on your spectacular performance this year. You and your team took on the stretch challenge of achieving Yen 2.5 billion in sourcing productivity for 1994. The final results are in and indicate an achievement of Yen 2.8B+! This is remarkable, but simply a testament to the skill and dedication of the GE-YMS sourcing team. It's great to have the best sourcing team in Asia in our organization. You continue to exceed our expectations and exhibit excellence year after year. I look forward to another stellar performance in 1995!"

Lesson

Every year from 1991 through 1995 we exceeded our commitment.

We had followed the Six Rules:
- *We committed to a dream – 8% sustained annual productivity.*
- *We believed in ourselves – We could DO it.*
- *We tried unconventional ideas – Supplier workouts in Japan.*
- *We made mistakes – Not everything worked well.*
- *We never gave up – Even when everyone else resisted us.*
- *We enjoyed the work and celebrated the success.*

CHAPTER 20

ON JOINING GEYMS BOARD

Ingenuity, plus courage, plus work, equals miracles...
Bob Richards. Pole Vaulter,
Two Times Olympic Gold Medalist

During 1995, Tsuji-san used to exhort me that I scored very low on his scale when it comes to self-promotion. Renu always concurred with him. The argument was that my contribution transcended sourcing globalization: My leadership had created a positive influence on the entire GEYMS Company. The management appreciated the bold experiments we undertook. People from other functions regarded my team as future leaders, and managers sought my counsel for their career moves. Therefore, I should be an ideal candidate to become an integral part of GEYMS management. Since we had contributed consistently to its bottom line (profitability) I would be able to generate the same in other areas by becoming a Director. "It is not just my desire to assume this position. It is in the interest of the entire GEYMS to have you elevated to Director", he said. Tsuji did not see me excited in promoting myself. It appeared that he took upon himself to speak to Goran Malm, then Chairman. I had no clue until Goran later told me in an unguarded moment in a bar that some leaders of my team had approached him with a request to promote me to a Director. He said he was astonished and wondered whether I was behind their lobbying efforts. When I asked him to disclose the names of those who went to him, he declined but said that I should be proud of such a team. Most of the times when people approached him, it was for backbiting their own leaders. Even today I have reasons to believe that it was Tsuji who moved behind the scene and created such lobbying efforts.

Effective January 1996, my job was expanded on two fronts. One was General Manager, Sourcing, GE Medical Systems, Asia. My charter was to integrate sourcing teams in Korea, Taiwan, China, and India. Tsuji succeeded me as General Manager, GE YMS Sourcing. The second was Global Champion for Global Growth-Market Sourcing. My challenge there was to develop suppliers in countries like eastern Europe, Mexico and developing Asia. GE management was pushing to not only buy products, subassemblies and services from these countries but to sell GE products and services to them as well. It was a 'win-win' scenario, and these countries were eager to learn and grow. In the new role, my reporting line was changed to a global level structure, to Serge Huot, Vice President, Manufacturing and Sourcing, and to Goran for Asia.

Serge was a great man to work with, a man of few words but a warm heart. I had never seen him losing temper. He was highly knowledgeable on manufacturing, its technologies, and operation management including Kanban systems among others. He sent a person from Paris, Pierre Claverie, to Tokyo to work as my assistant on a two-year assignment. Together we challenged both the assignments. Our key initiatives included stretching GEYMS sourcing team's potential by moving its best and brightest people to leadership positions. Yoshida was moved to Sourcing Manager for GE Tanaka X-ray (an affiliate of GE Medical Systems, Asia; GEMSA) in Saitama. Matsumoto, as mentioned earlier, went to

Beijing. Hosts of exchange and short assignments between GEYMS and eight other joint venture partners in Asia were made. Pierre was effective in coaching and sharing GE's best global sourcing practices. GEMSA sourcing teams were integrated into one 'boundaryless' team.

Pierre, Tsuji and myself worked on bringing global sourcing teams to Japan, China, Singapore, and India from the US and France. Vivek Paul, President, Wipro GE Medical Systems commented after such a meeting in Bangalore, India that we had trained them in organizing global events. It was their first exposure to this kind of practice. The global sourcing teams valued the Asian culture, its warm hospitality and they began to become knowledgeable on many good suppliers from whom they also started to buy. Mr. Kurata, my first boss at GEYMS used to say, "One thing the modern communication technology would find hard to accomplish is communicating your heart on electronic waves. Therefore, you've got to be physically there on the spot to touch, feel and experience. This moves the heart." When our American and European colleagues visited our suppliers in Asia they developed their own relationships. They invited suppliers to their facilities. Tsuji pioneered a trip for twenty strategic Japanese suppliers to visit the Milwaukee headquarters. Having visited our global facilities, they became so proud of being an important ally of the world's 'Number One Enterprise'. Tsuji and myself also visited Mexico, Czech and Poland in our pursuit of developing key suppliers but it appeared that they were not ready yet. Today in almost every country we visited then, GE Medical Systems has key suppliers. Our pioneering efforts did not go in vain.

On April 1st 1996, the Board of Directors, GE Yokogawa Medical Systems chaired by Goran Malm, approved my name to become a Director. The first person I talked to as soon as I received the news was Tsuji, and Renu was the second. It was my strong belief that Tsuji's relentless efforts made this dream of mine possible. Of course, in his modesty he never admitted that he was the true enabler to get me this coveted assignment. Upon accepting the directorship, I was asked about my vision. My response was,

"For GEMSA, it was to reach US$2 billion in sale by year 2000 and capture the number one market share in every country in Asia. GE Medical Systems in Asia was also on the move. New joint ventures were being formed. Each partner was aiming for value-added, knowledge based, and export-led growth. GEYMS had the basis for competitive advantage, as we were moving towards the twenty-first century. My vision, therefore, was that we capture and deploy our knowledge assets effectively in order to make a 'win-win' situation for GEYMS and our partners. We should be able to do this in Asia by creating a culture of urgency and commitment to quality. It would be possible to have this culture created by becoming an intra-company entrepreneur and going for this goal with everything we had. My motto was 'The impossible is possible, and we are determined to prove it toGEther."

Being on the Board gave me a broader perspective. I was exposed to every aspect of running a US$1 billion company and the complex issues the management had to deal with. Satisfying the customers unique needs with quality and timeliness, keeping employees motivated by stretching, challenging and appropriately rewarding them, ensuring integrity and compliance with laws, broadening knowledge of competitive moves, pursuing merger and acquisition possibilities, and, needless to say, meeting or exceeding operating plans every quarter were amongst the management's top priorities. Of course, my knowledge of sourcing also came in to play. From this vantage point, my thinking pattern was significantly widened. I started knowing answers to many questions, which used to nag me when I was running just the sourcing function. It was the pinnacle of my career.

Three years later, on my leaving GE, I wrote to Jack Welch.

'I firmly believe that I'm a living example of what you have been preaching consistently on GE being a global business enterprise: Being a citizen of India, living in Japan for 30 years and never ever had university level of education; yet I could rise to the Board of Directors of one of the most successful joint ventures, GE Yokogawa Medical Systems, to represent GE. This is only possible in GE.'

CHAPTER 21

SITTING ON THE OTHER SIDE OF FENCE

If there is a way to do it better... find it...
Thomas A. Edison

    The first casualty of my sitting on the Board was questioning or soul searching about my current job. I had followed only one track, sourcing, for twenty-five years. I started itching to try a new challenge like marketing or service. One of the main reasons was, during management discussions, sourcing did not have the limelight. It was sales, marketing or service that stole the show. I approached Goran to consider offering me other career opportunities. Goran hesitated because John Trani would never let him do so. John once told Renu that I had a bug. "Periodically, he wants to move to greener pasture." He believed I was good in sourcing and I had always been generously treated. Why on earth, then, would I think of doing something new? He could not comprehend my yearning for a different job.

    I kept on nudging Goran and finally in October 1996, he told me there was an opportunity to create a new business by directing my attention to a segment where GEYMS had not focused -

utilizing Japan's overseas development assistance (ODA) and Japanese export credits. However, he still needed to obtain clearance from Serge and John Trani before he committed it. Therefore, he wanted me to think whether it was of interest to me. I talked with Renu. She was concerned because in all my business life in Japan I had dealt with suppliers and now I could be wearing a sales suit and sitting on the other side of the fence. Would I be able to do it as effectively as I did for sourcing? However, she did not stop me. Goran, I always felt, was a visionary. He had an exceptionally sharp external sensory perception (ESP) in actualizing my potential. With John and Serge's blessings, Goran intoned that 'sky was the limit', and I had the capability to make it happen.

Effective January 1997, I moved into the new position as Director and General Manager, International Projects Division. Tsuji succeeded me in the sourcing function, wearing hats of GEYMS sourcing and GEMSA sourcing. In the newly created function, I had two very strong players, Jun Kimura and Yoko Takemura. They knew all facets of ODA process, had an excellent network with Japanese trading companies, consultants and officials at Japan International Cooperation Agency (JICA, the grant aid agency of Japanese government). Jun and Yoko created a vision to expand to global project financing by selling financial solutions to customers in developing countries. We raised our bar by challenging twice as high as the global growth of GE Medical Systems every year. In the first six months we bid on many aid-funded tenders but we did not win a single one. I started having doubts on my capability for selling. We were visiting many customers and partners, consultants and trading companies. Those efforts, however, did not bring awaited orders. I did remember a comment from Yamaguchi-san, Managing Director of GEYMS, "Sales is not an easy nut to crack. It requires a different set of skills. It would be advisable to return to sourcing."

The first order came in late June. We won a Syrian tender that Yoko had been pursuing. It exceeded US$1 million and was the success we needed desperately. It boosted our morale and restored the confidence of my team. On its heels came the next big win, twenty-eight units of portable á100 ultrasound scanners. It had a technical glitch though. Jiangsu Provincial Government in China, the customer, specifically requested equipment made in Japan but GEMS had moved the model's production from GEYMS (Japan) to Wipro GE Medical Systems in India. The contract award was on the verge of being nullified. We wanted to salvage it at any cost. Goran and Kawase-san, then President of GEYMS, were in New York. Jun Kimura was in Malaysia. The project owner, Hijikata, Yoko and myself were in the lobby of the customer's Tokyo hotel. We were given only six hours to determine whether we could produce those units in Japan. If our answer was negative the business would move to Toshiba. It was midnight. Yoko and Hijikata were communicating with Jun and I was on the phone seeking permission from Kawase-san to produce those units in Japan. We continued to explore possibilities with people in manufacturing. Around 3:00 a.m. we got the agreement to produce the units in Japan. We called the home of Mr. Ichikawa of C. Ito at 4:00 a.m., only two hours before the deadline, confirming that the scanners would indeed be produced by GEYMS facilities in Japan. Neither Ichikawa nor representatives from Jiangsu government could believe that this could happen with such lightening speed. The cooperation we got from everyone was of par excellence. Later in the execution phase, we offered the customer a choice of getting the equipment from Japan or from India, telling them that regardless of the manufacturing venue of GE products, quality would be the same and encouraged them to visit us in GEYMS Tokyo and Wipro GE in Bangalore, India to compare. The customer finally elected to have their order manufactured by Wipro GE in India. Including this deal, in 1996 we had orders aggregating Yen 100 million, and we closed 97 with Yen 530 million, a 500% growth indeed.

On October 1st, 1997 Masahiko Agata, a veteran of Export Import Bank of Japan, joined our team. It was Goran's idea to strengthen our team with an expert in international financing. Masahiko was instrumental in initiating two key strategies in addition to ODA business: Tapping multilateral development bank funds and leveraging structured financing for major projects like an oncology center in Azerbaizan. In April 1998 we won a Yen 400 million tender for a JICA-funded project in Bosnia and Herzegovina, a record for a single deal in our ODA-funded deals history, thanks to Jun and Wataru Takano's exceptional negotiation skills. For this project I personally visited its site in Bosnia, a country totally ravaged by the war - a truly pitiable sight all over. Later in the execution phase of the project, Wataru had to spend one month there to oversee the delivery. We closed 1998 with almost Yen 1 billion. We had indeed accomplished a '2X growth' in the two years. We were actively pursuing US$120 million prospects in twenty-two countries. On this job I traveled extensively - to countries like Israel (Jerusalem and Gaza Strip), Jordan (Amman), Russia (Moscow) and Indonesia, among others.

One achievement was to initiate and create a boundaryless behavior within GE Medical Systems. Measurements drive behavior and the pre-existing measurement scheme had created internal boundaries. Whenever we sold a project we received the sales credit and the local team got nothing. I had seven people on my team. It was a mission impossible to operate in twenty-two countries simultaneously. GE Medical Systems, however, had people on the ground in almost every country on earth. We needed their help in order to be successful. Therefore, we changed the measurements regime so that the recipient country would get the sales recognition as they did for their local sales. GEYMS management and GEMS Asia CFO, Joe Harlan, supported this change. Now we had 6,000 sales and service people around the globe in one seamless team. 'ToGEther in one boundaryless team, with a win-win attitude', we created a strategic difference versus our competitors. Under the new system we won the Bosnia and Herzegovina tender, for which a condition was to establish a service center in Sarajevo. Larry Johnston, President of GEMS Europe, led the European team and they did it in just three months. If we were to operate from Tokyo it would have taken three years and our success rate of making it an effective operation would have been significantly low. This kind of global best practice was only possible in GE. No single person is as smart as all of us together after all. GE became a preferred brand of ODA project drivers because of its global reach, its quality and service, which our competitors had difficulty in coming close to. GEYMS became a trusted partner for them because of its integrity and compliance to laws.

Keith Williams was President, GE Medical Systems Greater China (including Taiwan and Hong Kong). He helped me prepare operating plans and mid-range forecasts. I was not at all good at making crisp and persuasive presentations. I enjoyed being with him. His style of management was to create a vision and empower the team. He was absolutely unassuming and a down-to-earth leader. In 1997 he moved to Medtronic Asia Pacific, as its President. In Tokyo his home was the Hotel New Otani. I bumped into him one evening and thereafter we periodically met for dinner. Gradually, I started asking questions about Medtronic, a leading medical device company. One evening I casually asked whether I could have an opportunity to work with him. John Trani had left GE (becoming Chairman and CEO, Stanley Works) and Goran Malm had been elevated to Senior Vice President of GE (overseeing Asia). I felt there was a time for me to change too. Keith asked me to meet with Art Collins, COO, during his next trip to Tokyo. Events progressed smoothly and I was offered a position at Medtronic Asia, General Manager, Cardiac Surgery, Asia Pacific. On July

28th 1998, I made my intention known to Fujimori-san, GEMS Asia CEO, that I would retire from GE, after 27 years of service, effective December 31st, 1998. Renu was opposed to this move because of inherent risks involved. She always makes her opinion known but allows Adi and I to make our own decisions. By sheer coincidence, this day of submission of my resignation was the day Adi joined GE Power Systems in Atlanta.

On October 7th, Jack Welch was in Tokyo and I told him my plan. Astonished, he said he wanted me to manage entire GE's sourcing in China. He asked me whether it was my firm decision to retire. I responded in the affirmative. He recalled my 27 years in GE as the company's exciting time of growth. He wished me well.

On November 3rd midnight we received a call from Aditya. He was absolutely excited and his voice was shaking. I asked him to cool down. He said, "I shook Jack Welch's hand, it made my day! When he came to our division (Asia division), he asked one of my team members, Jeff, whether he speaks Japanese or not. Jeff said, "No I don't speak Japanese, but if I need I will ask Adi." What a coincidence. There are so many languages in Asia but he picked Japanese! Then José (Adi's boss and my friend) told him that I am Deven's son. He said that, "Oh you are his son. I cannot rage on Deven about sourcing anymore because he is retiring." Everyone on my team was amazed that my father knows Jack. Well people know you are retiring. He told me to say good luck to you!"

On December 18th, Masahiko Agata succeeded me as the General Manager, International Project Division. Subsequently he developed his team to the Asian center of excellence in global financing for projects, as part of GE Medical Systems Global Funding Operation, a function on a global platform.

On November 29th, 1998, Jack Welch responded to my note.

Dear Deven, Thank you for your special note and for all your many contributions to GE over the years. Your 27 years have been exciting times in the company and you have played a significant role in every job you had. Your last one (International Products Division) was sure unique, as were your contributions to it.

Deven, I enjoyed meeting with Aditya. He looks like a very promising young man. Congratulations!

I wish you the very best in your new life. Enjoy every minute of it ... you sure earned it.

All the best,

Jack.

CHAPTER 22

MEDTRONIC... MY SECOND LIFE

I don't think there is any other quality so essential to success of any kind as the quality of perseverance. It overcomes almost everything, even nature...

John D. Rockefeller

After spending twenty-seven years with GE in mind and body, moving to Medtronic on January 11,1999 (easy to remember in Japanese calendar, *Heisei* 11 *nen* 1 *gatsu* 11 *nichi*) was with mixed feelings. I was sad to leave GE but excited to challenge a different culture, products and face the customers, primarily cardiac surgeons. It was refreshing. Keith Williams, President and CEO, Medtronic Asia Pacific, welcomed me personally and introduced me to Japan Cardiac Surgery Team headed by a young and promising leader, Atsuji Iwasa. One of the first actions Keith recommended was dropping me in the ocean, where I had to find my way of survival by going to a heart valve training program in Niigata for young doctors to practice our tissue heart valves on pigs. Dynamic leaders Satoru Yamamoto and Tada were in charge. It was a two-day event. Thereafter, Satoru and myself flew to Kansai Airport, Bangkok and St. Antonio, Texas for a Society of Thoracic Surgeons (STS) conference. During the show I met key leaders of the entire cardiac surgery team in Asia. The person who helped me was Goh Khoon-seng, a Singaporean, who knew everyone there, their background, history and other details. I asked Goh to help me organize a lunch, while we were in the US, for the entire Asia cardiac surgery team. It was a fine opportunity to meet the leaders from India, China, southeast Asia, Australia, Korea and, of course, from Japan on one table, and, that too, in my first week on the job.

Knowing Goh was an instant click. He became my brain from that moment. His creativity and networking was *par excellence*. His multifaceted knowledge of cardiac surgeons, products, distribution systems across Asia and the US was of immense help. He was always beside me to help. Later on Cecilia Koh, also from Singapore, joined our team and the three of us almost changed the map of Asia in the following twenty-four months. With Keith's blessings, we created a vision in Asia for cardiac surgery to nearly triple by 2005.

Another person who guided me was Nam Lee. He was leading the neurological business for Asia. Nam was also highly knowledgeable in his field and very compassionate.

In the first few weeks I made the following three observations:
- The Japan team was highly privileged.
- Asia was divided into six regions.
- The 'rest of Asia', other than Japan, was a low priority for the senior management of Medtronic in the US.

The Japan team was pampered because their profitability was high. They never felt that they were a part of Asia. Meanwhile, the teams in India, southeast Asia, China, Korea, Australia and New Zealand, and Japan were fragmented and disjointed and only country-focused. All regions had excellent growth opportunities but there was not much sharing of best practices and communication between them. The management did recognize the potential of the 'rest of Asia', but the reality was that Japan was contributing to Medtronic's profitability and, hence, dominated the company's attention as its strategic importance. It was Keith who was changing their paradigm. He took upon himself to persuade Bill George, CEO to substantially increase investment and focus in developing Asia.

In the first 3 months, Goh and myself worked on the blueprint to facilitate all the regional teams working together to make the cardiac surgery team in Asia as one united team: To share knowledge and ideas from each region, to learn to benefit from each other, and to exploit the advantage of Asia having brilliant cardiac surgeons by moving them around in Asia to help each region for a growth in sales. The first step was to initiate a weekly e-mail 'APCS interactive forum'. Its objective was to communicate the key developments of each region on a weekly basis. The immediate feedback was that people started talking to each other directly on the subjects of their interest. It started gaining attention from surprising quarters like from people in Minneapolis headquarters. They asked me to include their names on the mailing list. Within a few months I felt that we all were almost on the same wavelength on most of the issues. The biggest benefit was that country and cultural barriers were broken down. Later, Goh and Cecilia initiated a quarterly APCS newsletter focusing on new products and key events of each country. It became not only popular in Asia but around the globe because of it's quality and high level of contents. The Asia team became knowledgeable and so did our counterparts in Europe and the US.

We created an Asia Pacific Perfusion Systems Board. It was an experiment to bring perfusion systems business teams together transcending countries' boundaries and was chaired by Patrick Williams, a young and enthusiastic leader from Sydney. Our objective was to stretch his potential by driving forward the business horizon. Patrick conducted weekly calls to all six regions in Asia, in which teams were asked to bring three issues of the week for which they needed support. To illustrate, if Japan had an issue, India might have a solution, and similarly if China had a problem, Australia might be of help. By working together, we enhanced the cooperation across the entire region. Sometimes we even invited business managers from US to listen to our issues and help us. They would hear one voice, an Asia voice, and it was easy for them to help us quickly resolve issues.

The highlight of my two years with Medtronic was to move top cardiac surgeons around Asia. We invited Dr. Matsuda (the first surgeon in 30 years to perform a heart transplant in Japan) to Seoul to give a lecture and demonstrate his technique at Medtronic Heart Valve Training. He was so popular that leading surgeons from Seoul and nearby cities were standing in a queue to meet or listen to him. It was Dr. Matsuda's second trip to Korea since the first fifteen years before, and he was very surprised on visits to places like Samsung Hospital, which he described as one of the best he had ever seen. We also brought Dr. M.R. Girinath from Apollo Hospital in Madras to Changsha, China. It was his first trip to China. We celebrated his 60th birthday there. He invited Chinese doctors to his hospital to implant heart valves in Indian patients. It was Keith's vision that Medtronic Asia Pacific not only be perceived as a business entity but as cultivating the legacy by providing hands-on experience to young surgeons who did not have ample opportunities in their own countries.

Dr. Hitoshi Kasegawa went to Madras and then to Hyderabad, India to provide heart valve training to Indian doctors. Joining him was Dr. Richard Chard from Sydney. His first cultural shock was the 'punctuality' of time. He had been told that the demonstration would start from 6:30 p.m. Naturally, he arrived there in the hall at 6:15 p.m., but, to his surprise, the venue was empty. Neither was the room ready for demonstration nor any person there. He thought he was at a wrong place. He enquired and was told that the venue was correct but in India, generally things did not happen on time. He was requested to take rest in his hotel suite until called. Around 8:00 p.m., he still had no call and of course no one came to pick him up. He became restless and went to the venue again, by himself. He then saw that tables were being set and a few doctors had finally started coming in. Finally, at 9:00 p.m. the session started and went on as late as to 11:30 p.m. followed by dinner! However, in the end, he admired the quality of discussion and professionalism of the doctors.

Dr. James Wong from Singapore visited Cho Ray Hospital in Ho Chi Minh City. It was an instant success not only because he was a very skilled surgeon but also because he is very personable and the hospital staff just loved him. We brought India's two leading surgeons, Drs. K.M. Cherian and Muralidharan, close to Drs. Matsuda and Kasegawa in Singapore thru informal discussion. In Xian, China, we had by far the largest heart valve training. More than 170 doctors trained in a wet-lab with pig hearts. Doctors from Japan, Singapore and Australia, along with their counterparts from China, worked together to provide this unique learning experience. Dr. Steven Bolling from Michigan, an authority on valve repair, came to Bangkok. He conducted a live surgery in Ramathibodhi Hospital where almost 100 doctors were watching with keenest interest on outside monitors. Dr. Bolling was so impressed with the modesty of Asian people that he offered to return to Asia at least three times a year.

Goh and Cecilia organized our first APCS team business session in Phuket, Thailand in December 1999. Not only the senior management including Bob Guezuraga, Senior Vice President, and others from Medtronic headquarters but also our key distributors from every country attended the session. It was our attempt to show Bob Asia as one critical mass which presented tremendous opportunities for the company to invest in R& D and manufacturing, and sales potential as well. 'Medtronic needed to look at Asia where the next wave of growth was imminent because 50% of the world population resides there. Asian anatomy and needs are different and so are the prices.'

Dr. Saw Huat Seong in Singapore sought our help in putting Asia onto the cardiac surgery map by initiating an annual seminar, named MULU Rafflesia Heart Valve Symposium, in August 2000 as an annex to Rocky Mountains Symposium in the US. The location was inside a deep rain forest, a very beautiful and quiet place. Because of his personal influence, Dr. Saw was able to attract top global surgeons from Europe, Japan and US. It was such an impressive gathering that our Director for southeast Asia operation, David Jolly, committed to continue our sponsorship for the next five years. It was a seminal event.

On our internal side, in order to raise the future leadership in Asia we sent Iwasa-san on a two-year assignment to Medtronic headquarters in Minneapolis. Goh received coveted management recognition, 'Star of Excellence', for his superb contribution to promote cardiac surgery in Asia. With these initiatives came the growth. Revenue increased 25% in 2000 and 23% in 2001. Earnings Before Interest and Tax (EBIT) more than doubled in 2000 and we attained a 'One Asia Pacific Cardiac Surgery Team'; simultaneously fostering the human resources development.

In the midst of all this I had three nagging concerns. My knowledge of heart valves, perfusion systems and minimally invasive coronary bypass was very low, while those products were of very high technologies. This was reflected in my inability to talk intelligently with cardiac surgeons on the state-of-art products and how they applied to human anatomy. My role was reduced to just a cheerleader. Another problem was that I hated to visit hospitals, watching the patients in operation theatres, seeing their body's cut and the blood. My first test came when Keith arranged for me to go to Prince of Wales Hospital in Sydney. The doctor warned me that if I was not used to seeing human blood, chances were there that I might become dizzy. His advice was that if that happened please make sure not to fall flat on the patient. Although I did not fall flat on the patient, I could not eat a meal for the following three days. It was indeed an experience of immense anguish.

Nitin Shah, Managing Director of Medtronic, India, recognized my concerns. He told me that in order to do justice to my assignment I needed to have a working knowledge on anatomy, disease and technology so that I would be able to communicate with cardiac surgeons at progressively deeper levels. Medtronic was spending 10% of its budget for new products development, the lifeline of the company. Doctors were curious to know our latest offerings. Therefore, Nitin personally prepared for me a curriculum that included learning basic knowledge of human anatomy and our products plus, competitive offerings in the market place. He put his entire cardiac surgery team to train me: Sanjay Date for heart valves, Anil Mankodi for perfusion systems and Ramesh Lakshman for minimally invasive coronary bypass. In addition, he arranged for me to visit hospitals. I went to Coimbatore in south India. Dr. Muralidharan, one of the top three surgeons in south India, was to train me for a week on implanting mechanical heart valves, not only of Medtronic but also of competitive models. He performed eight surgeries every day. His professional fingers and brisk speed reminded me of an artist drawing a painting on the canvas. Every move was so majestic, whether slitting the body or suturing the wounds. After seeing forty surgeries in one week, I felt I would soon become a sick person and I could not relish food during that week. Dr. Muralidharan advised that images of operation theaters and patients would soon become a mechanical routine of my daily life and, therefore, I should just hang on in there.

In August 2000, Keith was ready for a bigger job, Senior Vice President for Spine and Neurology. It was an over $1.0 billion business. He had left an outstanding legacy from his three years. In 1997, Asia was amid an economic crisis and Medtronic Asia Pacific's turnover was $240 million. He delivered a 94% increase to $466 million, developing a strong leadership team - mostly of Asians. He grew by stretching their potential. David Jolly, President southeast Asia, came from a sales territory in Perth, Australia. Hiroshi Kudo rose through ranks to become President, Medtronic Japan. Keith initiated an 'Asia Pacific Management Development Program' to develop the next generation of leadership within Asia, familiarizing them with the unique culture of other Asian countries and with the business skills, acumen and leadership needed for success. His approach included such unique ideas as bringing them to a hot spring bath in Sapporo, an experience to remember for people from India and southeast Asia. Indeed, he changed the Medtronic Asia map.

Chuck Brynelsen, Keith's successor, apparently had a different vision and expectation from the Asia team. During my very first face-to-face interview, he told me that a leader of my level who did not have knowledge on Medtronic products and could not represent Medtronic effectively to the community of surgeons was not qualified to be in the job. He challenged me by saying that if I could not pass his test on Medtronic products, I would be fired, giving me until April 2001. I started seeing the writing on the wall.

In Spring 2000, Renu was itching to diversify her activities towards areas other than cooking. Sachiko Inomata, Associate

Editor at Shibata Shoten, who had edited her two books, introduced her friend, Sato-san, to her. Sato-san was keen to start a neo-Indian style café. He invited Renu to join in the venture. He already had two partners in this project. Renu, although very conservative in thinking, agreed quickly because she did not want to stick to the traditional Indian restaurant either. Events moved briskly. The four partners launched a beautiful café named 'Renu Arora' at a very posh location in Aoyama, Tokyo. The ambience was uniquely neo-Indian with open space under a tent and the bar separately attached. It was spacious and young women just loved it. Renu and I felt so good that we kept on investing to the tune of 20 million Yen. Its opening was equally superb. More than 500 friends and her students graced it. In the first two months sales were very high but two issues became critical for its survival. First, we could not find good chefs who could master Renu's uniquely delicious dishes quickly, while the clientele depended on the quality of taste and its consistency, the same quality could not be delivered to repeat customers' requests. Naturally the number of customers declined. The second problem was one of the partners started pulling out his share without the others knowledge. It created a trust issue. Finally we were forced to close the restaurant on December 28th, just after four months from its opening. Our 20 million Yen investment just evaporated.

An alternative was proposed by the other two partners to sue the partner who had withdrawn their investment. Sato-san wanted us to join them in the legal battle but our benefactor, Mr. Koichi Inasawa, also our attorney who had been involved in this project from day one, counseled us against going to court. He told us that we had a very strong case but that we should consider the cost of filing and fighting a case. It would take more than a year, even if everything went smoothly, and during that period our peace at home, emotional balance and family life would be ruined. Would it be worthwhile going this route? Sato-san went to court alone.

He was persistent. Later we came to know that he spent at least as much as his initially investment fighting the case. We did not keep track of this and do not know what its ultimate outcome was, but Renu was completely broken down. She did not want to continue her classes. She said she had no desire to work any more. Her feelings were absolutely understandable.

After Keith moved to the US, the atmosphere in Medtronic Asia team was turning from open and consensual to secretive. People started playing a kind of guesswork as to what Chuck wanted to accomplish, rather than openly arguing and understanding what should be done. His vision was not clear. Further, Bob Guezuraga, Senior Vice President for the Cardiac Surgery Business, felt that I might not be an appropriate leader for such a high tech business. On December 19th, he told me that he liked my positive attitude, my drive for results and my building an excellent team in Asia. I could be proud of these accomplishments and proud that we had always met our goals but he did not see much progress in my product and clinical related knowledge, hence, reluctantly, he would relieve me from the job of Vice President for Asia Pacific Cardiac Surgery. On January 9th, 2001 Chuck notified to me that Medtronic Asia Pacific elected not to renew my contract.

Lesson

A great pleasure in life is doing what people say you cannot do.

■

CHAPTER 23

IN THE VALLEY OF ABYSS

*Our greatest glory is not in never falling,
but in rising every time we fall...*
Confucius

The weight of my dismissal from Medtronic made its imprint felt. The first lesson was that an unparallel string of our success of 22 years was not a guarantee for the future although I probably wished and acted that this were not so. It was a very rude awakening, these two colossal losses: Renu's venture evaporated with 20 Million Yen and my being fired brought our lives to virtually a standstill.

I had to take the leadership in bringing semblance of order in our otherwise emotionally distraught state of affairs. It took me three weeks to decide what could be the best scenario. It was in my hands.

Priority # 1: Provide emotional support to Renu in order to bring her back on her feet.

Priority # 2: Keep Aditya out of the fray so that he could concentrate on his job and live peacefully in the US.

With these two priorities, the choice, it seemed to me, was to keep my own emotional disaster close to my heart and pretend business as usual to maintain the facade that I still had my job. I encountered many difficulties in keeping my on-the-job posture. The first one among them was the nature of my job. It entailed travel about 50% of the time but now I was not traveling. When Renu questioned why I did not travel, I had to come up with some logical excuse. 'I obtained approval of my boss to let me operate from Tokyo for a few months so that I could spend more time with you.' She appreciated and smiled.

My usual routine was that I still went to 'office'. Therefore, I dressed up every morning and left home around 8:00 a.m. with my lunch packet containing very delicious sandwiches (incidentally, my lunch packet was very famous in the office. Everyone used to peek and wanted to have a taste of it. My secretary, Sato-san, would snatch away the sandwiches with the comment that I had an access to them and I could eat them anytime I wanted). Although I left the home in the morning, the question was where to go. I would walk aimlessly. I would sit in lobbies of various hotels just to while away the time reading the newspaper and drinking tea. Lunch would be eaten in the park. Sometimes I visited office to pick up the mail. I sought the cooperation from Sato-san that in the event Renu and other friends called me please respond that I was temporarily out of office. In the evening, Sato-san was courteous enough to give me a run down on the callers, which I followed up later. I just hated this 'acting'. I was fed up. I wanted to run away - but where to? Looking at Renu's state of mind, which was returning to normalcy, I did not want to risk this cherished improvement. Therefore, howsoever unacceptable my situation was, I had to stick to this decision. My #1 priority was to make Renu smile so that she could return to teach Cooking again.

During this 'darkest period of my life', I lost sight of the future. I was fifty-eight. There was no possibility of getting a job in Japan with the income level, privileges and status that I enjoyed during my days in GE and Medtronic. I was completely tormented. Everything in my personal life was crumbling before my eyes. It was indeed a very hopeless situation. Sitting in restaurants and drinking tea did not inspire me to even read the daily newspapers, although I was still an avid reader and had my own library. I did not know what to do and whom I should talk to. The only positive thing was that Renu gained her original composure. It took her almost four months.

One day I received a call from Yvonne Moore, Vice President, Human Resources, Medtronic Asia Pacific, informing me about my being enrolled in a leading global placement agency. It was counseling persons who were looking for alternative opportunities. Since Japan was going through restructuring, people above forty years of age were the candidates for their second life support programs. It was basically addressed to low performers, however. Most Japanese had worked for only one company. They were at loss to seek opportunities. Agencies like the one I was recommended to, provided counseling for those people and I did not see myself that way. Their primary job was to listen, boost the client's morale and guide them to alternative opportunities. It was especially hard on these people because they joined their respective companies when Japan was in a growth mode. When young they had a very bright future; all they had to do was to be loyal to their employers. After having served 20-plus years they suddenly faced an unforeseen fate. Almost everyone was going through similar feelings to reconcile with the stark reality. Watching them made me even sicker. I felt that the last thing I needed in my life was to stand in a queue with these dropouts. All my working life I consistently achieved A+. I was an achiever. I was in a different league. I had no comparison. The reality, however, was that whatever my credentials, what I was basing my comparison with these people was history. I had to accept the reality of today, I was one of them. We were on the same boat.

As luck had it, I happened to be counseled by a young but wise lady, Hiromi Nezaki. She allowed my suppressed feelings to vent out. I rambled for hours and hours. She patiently listened, and thereafter she asked me to tell her about my family, achievements in career, track record, hobbies, friends circle and other areas, which I was proud of. She asked me to visit her two days later as she needed time to digest all the information and create my profile. During my second meeting, she said that it was the test to my professionalism built over thirty years but boiled down to only two choices; sink with it and get lost in the wilderness, or face reality as it is and build the future. The choice was entirely mine. My being fired from Medtronic was a tiny blip in my otherwise distinguished career. I should not let this incident assume a larger-than-life proportion. "Use it as the springboard to swing into new phase of life." I should remember that how far you fall is unimportant; the height of your bounce is what counts.

During this time, the London office director of Nezaki-san's consulting firm, Stuart Walkey, happened to be in Tokyo for a two-day visit. She arranged a two-hour interview with him. "You will be a different person. Don't miss this fine opportunity", she said. I had no difficulty in committing two hours, as I had no constraints on my time. Meeting with Stuart, as Nezaki-san predicted, was a life-changing experience. During our session, which lasted for five hours, instead of two, he did not even spend a second on my being fired from Medtronic. His entire focus was on my 58 years life full of the finest experiences, courageous decisions and spectacular achievements. He extolled my so much packing in such a short span of 58 years that I should truly be proud of myself. "This one fact you should deeply ingrain into your brain. Whenever your heart starts sinking in, close your eyes and switch on the screen. Watch your top 3 or 5 accomplishments in technicolor. Relish your success vividly. Do not let negative thoughts creep in. You have led such a colorful life that negative thoughts have no place whatsoever."

Stuart then rewrote my CV. Going through it, I could not believe that I accomplished so much. He took the same facts, without embellishing, but the magic that made a difference was in the way facts were organized and composed.

Stuart has become my mentor on life. Even today, if I have a major issue, he comes back in less than a few hours with his philosophical but practical gems of inspiration. He is always with me. He fought for me with two ministers in one country, where he asked me to apply for an opportunity, to consider my candidacy. Nezaki-san and Stuart are very loyal persons. Nezaki-san used to tell me that we three are friends-for-life. It is so true. We are very close today and will continue forever. It was their constant dose of encouragement that I could claw back from the valley of abyss.

Lesson

'Use your failure as the springboard to swing into a new phase of life'. Remember that how far you fall is unimportant; the height of your bounce is what counts.

CHAPTER 24

AN OPPORTUNITY THAT REWROTE MY LIFE

An entrepreneur is essentially a visualizer and an actualizer...
He can visualize something, and when he visualizes it
he sees exactly how to make it happen...

Robert L. Schwartz

Back in 1997, John Trani, my former boss at GE, became Chairman and Chief Executive Officer, The Stanley Works based in New Britain, Conn. Boasting a 160-year history, Stanley is a global manufacturer of high quality tools and hardware goods for professional, industrial and home improvement use. At that time it's annual sales were $2.5 billion. I called him to congratulate and wished him the best. John then told me that he would need me as his sourcing leader in Asia. He, however, was not sure of the timing; it could be a two-year wait. During early 1998, I visited him in New Britain. He spent significant time with me taking me through the details of Stanley, the challenges he was facing in turning around its culture, management discipline and creating a passion for change. It was obvious that he was genuinely interested in having me on his leadership team in Asia. However, neither could he make an offer nor did he nail down the precise timing. I believed it was because of his contractual obligation with GE.

Meanwhile, I signed up with Keith Williams to join Medtronic effective January 1st, 1999. It so happened that on December 28th, 1998, while we were vacationing in the Bahamas, a letter was redirected to me from Tokyo. It was from John Trani informing me that he was ready to make an offer. This was a pickle. I called Claudia, John's executive assistant, whom I had the privilege to know since 1990. She had always been very nice to me. On my mentioning of my move to Medtronic, she responded with great astonishment, "You bombed me out, Deven. John has been counting on you. How could you do this to him when you knew he needed the support of his loyal and trusted friends?" She did gracefully recommend me to speak to John. A big boy, he would understand as to why I elected to go down Medtronic route although he might not agree with my action, I thought. However, talking to John was a very different story. He was not only upset but also banged down his phone on me. Being a grateful recipient of his generosity and strategic leadership support for almost eighteen years I had no desire to be in his bad books. Therefore, I decided to seek his blessings on my move to Medtronic. He refused to take my call five times. I sought Claudia's help. John, finally, told me that his doors were always open should I desire to join Stanley.

As the saying goes, neither permanent friends nor foes but only our interests, I thought to cash in that check in April 2001. Still he was mad but the intensity was not that strong. I gathered that he still liked me. His warmth had the likeness of the prodigal son returning home after a detour. He asked me to lead the Stanley Buying Office in Taipei, Taiwan. The catch was that I had to move to Taipei and launch a brand new sourcing operation in China because manufacturing always gravitates to low cost countries, and China was the logical choice.

During the first week of May, Renu and I visited Atlanta to consult with Aditya as to how we should proceed on finding him a bride, preferably from India. During that week, under the pretext of visiting Medtronic headquarters in Minnesota, I went to Stanley headquarters in New England to meet John. The Stanley management team interviewed me formally. An offer was made to me to become the President, Asia Sourcing Operations of The Stanley Works. I was required to make my home in Taipei and then move to Shanghai or Shenzhen depending on our supplier base.

My next challenge was to break the news of leaving Medtronic and joining Stanley to Renu and Aditya. I had lived all my working life in Japan with Renu. Although there were business trips of considerable length and they were quite frequent, it was the very first time I had to move my home base outside Japan, ever since we had settled there. I needed to persuade Renu to live in Tokyo alone, as there was no way that she, with her own successful cooking business, would move to Taipei with me. Here again, I seeked Nezaki-san and Stuart's counsel. Stuart, being a gem, gave me three nuggets of wisdom:

- Utilize our temporary parting as an opportunity to spend quality time together during our reunion. It will blossom our love and understanding. We would recognize each other's value and company in different light. It would be a new start,
- Spend a week together when either she comes to Taipei/China or I visit Tokyo every 12 weeks. Shorter intervals would be better. Do not bring work home during that week as far as possible
- This is a global trend. Efficient executives are in short supply. Therefore, consider that I was moving into the major league.

Equipped with these thoughts, I spoke with Renu and Aditya. As I expected both were very angry. Renu, in particular, was blunt, saying that if I had the guts to hide being fired from Medtronic so long what else had I been hiding from them? Aditya's reaction was sober, "Dad, we did not earn your trust yet to share your pains. You didn't believe that we could absorb the two great family setbacks at the same time." The next two weeks were a nightmare. Gradually, both of them appreciated that my intentions were not misplaced, although perhaps the approach should have been different. They both were grateful to the fact that I had an opportunity to excel in my professional field of sourcing because Mr. Trani was gracious to embrace me. Renu advised me to focus 2000% on my job. Visiting a country where the environment and culture were different, is one aspect but living there would pose different challenges. It would be the second move in life - the first 1965 when I came to Japan. She went to the extent that, "You need not worry about me at all as we had many good friends around in Tokyo to take care."

On June 4th, 2001 I moved to Taipei. Gary Cooper was the founding father of Stanley Buying Services. This group was responsible for sourcing for Stanley's eight business divisions. The product lines were doors, hydraulic tools, air tools, hand tools, mechanic tools and fastening systems. Gary was a 36-year veteran at Stanley. His father also served Stanley for thirty-six years and the topper was that his grandfather equally had a 36-year service record with the Stanley. Over the three generations, the Coopers had put in 108 years of service. In my sixty-two years of life, Gary is the only person I know of with a family history of loyalty and attachment to one company. It made my task more daunting to succeed him. In fact, for a few months the entire office in Taipei did not like me. Even my secretary, Valery Chueh, told that she hated me because I took away Mr. Cooper's job. During the assembly for the formal announcement, most of the team was in tears to see Gary being 'demoted'. I made a promise to myself that I would preserve Gary's image and dignity, respecting his loyalty to Stanley and to the Taipei team as well. I did not move into his office and never once sat on his chair, although Gary offered me to do so several times.

On June 9th, I received a call from Bombay that our dear *Mummiji* (Renu's mother) passed away after a prolonged illness that had forced her to be bedridden for almost twenty years. I still believe that she waited to see that I had a secure job and we became happy after our traumatic experiences. She had always been inspiring all of us. Her heart had an extraordinary thing called love and everyone around her felt its depth, the delight and the ecstasy of it. It was of course a big loss, but having seen her own plight, we did believe that she was also relieved.

John asked me to visit him in the third week of June to give me a charter, his five commandments. They were:

- Build a professional sourcing team in China.
- Develop a new supplier base in China while simultaneously moving the current Taiwanese supplier base to China.
- Deliver 10%+ productivity every year.
- Phase down the Stanley Taiwan sourcing operation and move to China in three years.
- Look for M & A or joint venture opportunities with suppliers in areas where Stanley did not have in-house expertise like cutting devices.

My challenge was set to deliver $10 million in cost savings (productivity) in the second half of 2001, meaning in the next 26 weeks. It was a tall order. However, having known John for close to twenty years, I knew where my priority should be. It was to deliver $10 million in the remainder of 2001. The rest was just a conversation. John did give some ideas, one of them being to meet

Judy Lee, President, Test Rite group of companies, in Taipei. Test Rite was supplying us US$ 40 million on an annualized basis. John's guideline to me was to negotiate 12-18% price reduction on the entire buy.

On return to Taipei, I consulted Gary and the buying team. It sounded like Greek to them. They did not know how and where to start. Everyone thought that it was mission impossible. Gary told me that neither the team had skills nor reconciling techniques to link savings with corporate accounting and it was my first challenge. The clock was ticking.

The first step was to hire a finance manager who would also be our productivity driver. My Medtronic contact recommended Maria Yang, a dynamic person, who was a perfect match to the job profile I was looking for. Maria joined us on September 14th. From September 17th, we launched 'Focus 10' project, a drive to deliver $10 million savings in 2001. Before Maria came on board, I was meeting with the team every Monday morning at 9:30 a.m. to seek their valued input. I told them to focus on three actions:

- Bring in any idea by which cost could be saved quickly,
- Make an action plan for the week with who does what by when,
- Report the result of last week's actions in real $ cost savings.

It was a totally new concept for the team.

I sensed that Gary was not comfortable with this focused effort. We both discussed as to how we could divide our responsibilities. He suggested building a professional sourcing team in China. His recommendation appealed to me. He virtually moved to Shanghai for the next 4 months until his retirement in December 2001.

At John's recommendation, we arranged a dinner meeting with Judy Lee of Test Rite. Tony Ho, her husband and the Chairman of the company, was gracious enough to join us. Judy, an entrepreneur, started trading in tools business in 1978. Test Rite's quality of products and services and on-time execution was *par excellence*. So was her competitive pricing. Her business relations with Wal-Mart and other retail stores in many countries had grown rapidly. Tony Ho had diversified the business into retail. I believe they were US$1 billion-plus business spread in 23 countries. Judy was ranked Number 9 in 2000 among the female business leaders in entire Taiwan. For her 'impossible is always possible.'

During our first meeting, I thought it would be a no-no to discuss business because I was told that she wanted to welcome me to Taipei as Stanley's representative. I was therefore a little hesitant to bring business topics up amidst the pleasantries we were exchanging and while enjoying the fine food. After dinner was over, I requested her to pardon me to talk some business. Judy, an affable, polite person with an easy-to-get-along demeanor, encouraged me to make my request. Not only did she listen but also she understood where I was coming from. It did not, of course, mean 'Yes' to everything I asked for. She did say, "Let's talk next week and see how much support I can possibly give." Her philosophy had left an indelible image on my mind. She said that it was in Test Rite's business interest to keep our customers competitive. If Stanley is competitive it is a sign of her enterprise's growth.

She impressed me to the extent that I connected her on the phone with John right from the dinner table. John was quick to approve my request for a 12% off for regular shipments and 18% price reduction for the tools and hardware goods needed for Christmas promotions. During the next week we agreed with Test Rite upon 7% and 11% respectively. It netted to Stanley little over $1 million in saving. We had an excellent start towards our $10 million saving drive.

Dealing with Judy was fun and an experience of a lifetime. Her down-to-earth leadership had a very different perspective. She always put herself in the customer's shoes and never argued with them. Business discussions were heated and emotional at times but the atmosphere was always friendly. Stanley was not performing well in consecutive quarters, the third and fourth quarters of 2002 and the first quarter of 2003. We needed a very special support on our purchases for the first quarter 2003. Judy supported Stanley by providing cash discounts. It simply reflects Judy's loyalty to the customer. She always stands behind customers in their difficult times.

Maria made the process transparent, easy to understand and numbers visible. Every Monday morning the entire sourcing team saw the results in $s, year-to-date and how much to go for. In the middle of October the team started feeling the warmth. Sensing that it might be doable, they started looking into possibilities. Creative juices started flowing in and excitement was building. Under Maria's disciplined and consistent follow-up the team was responding so that in November I felt our target might be achieved. From that point on there was no return. Our excitement was at a peak. In the first week of December Maria told me in confidence that at the prevailing pace we might exceed John's $10 million challenge but, she added, "Please keep it under your hat." However, I wanted to share it with Gary, and called him in Shanghai. He could not believe that the team was turning in a whopping US$ 13.7 million. John liked what he saw. We were a numbers-driven team, not only meeting but also exceeding the commitment. His reward was to grant a special fund for the entire team to celebrate in Bali, Indonesia.

Gary was very active in China. We planned to hire 40 engineers and specialists, 15 in Shanghai and 25 in Shenzhen because we had more suppliers based in those areas. We received almost 2,000 applications. Screening all those was a challenge of monumental proportion. He needed a human resource manager so we hired Lillian Yeh. She was the best HR manager I had ever worked with in my career. She was dynamic and creative. Her enthusiasm was just contagious. By November, we had the team lined up in China. Gary's fine efforts resulted also in arranging professional trainers, Jerry Kardas and Gopi Gopalan. We had consistent support from Lian Cheng Ping and his HR manager Lily Ge throughout the entire process. Cheng Ping, President for Stanley China, was personally involved in every facet of our undertaking and ensured that we had a great start.

The man who taught the tools and hardware business was Alex Du, my sourcing manager for hand tools. Alex was not only an expert on tools business but on suppliers, customers and their merchandizing needs as well. During the initial stages, John asked me several questions on suppliers, business trends and competitive intelligence in China, and it was Alex who drafted the answers which I rewrote, not changing the contents but just retouching english to reflect my flavor.

After Gary's retirement, we formed the management team with Maria, Lillian, Alex, Valery, Richard Zhou (whom I scouted from GE Medical China to manage engineering and quality) and myself. We had monthly staff meetings at rotating venues of Taipei, Taichung, Shanghai and Shenzhen.

My next challenge was to blend the two teams - Taiwan and China – across the Straits so that we could work together as one. Lillian worked tirelessly to bring the two teams together. She initiated programs to develop their english communication skills. She launched 'Leadership Development Training Course' with professional help from Jeff Chen, President Stanley Asia Manufacturing Operations. Before moving to China, it appeared to me that Taiwan, Hong Kong and mainland China shared the same culture, but I was absolutely wrong. To paraphrase George Bernard Shaw, China and Taiwan are divided by the common heritage. Today they are like water and oil. Even their written characters are different. Taiwan maintains traditional style characters, whereas the mainland has simplified characters. It was my continuous challenge to bring them on the same table to agree on any issue. I used to tell them that, thanks to Stanley, a global enterprise, this management team had the opportunity to rise above petty issues between Taiwan and mainland so that we should, and could, focus on problems and strive for the best solution we can come up in Stanley's best interest. Lillian worked hard to bring Richard to Taiwan. It took Lillian six months and significant expenses to have it realized. It was a rare achievement to see this happen in the climate where the policies of both governments encourage the people's traffic overwhelmingly directed from Taiwan to China (90% to China).

John invited me to dinner on January 2nd, 2002. Such invitations were only to seek commitments on more than what you excelled in delivering in the preceding year. His logic was simple. If you could deliver $13.7 million in 26 weeks, you should be able to deliver $27 million in the 52 weeks of 2002. He told me that it would be easy to remember if we could settle at a rounded number of $30 million. I negotiated down to $26 million with a stretch to $30 million. It meant that my firm commitment to John was to deliver $26 million in cost savings in 2002 but I should stretch my team to go for $30 million target. If we failed to deliver $30 million we would not be penalized. He would track every quarter so that our numbers be linked with the quarterly balance sheet of entire Stanley. Therefore, we decided to track for ourselves, $2.5 million for the first quarter, $6.5 million for the second, $10 million for the third, and $7 million for the fourth. It should be reflected in the shipping pattern, peaking in the second and the third quarters. The topper was that he had me pay the dinner bill -

He made my life so spicy that I owed him at least that meal," was his affectionate remark.

We toiled to hit and exceed our quarterly commitments. After we posted the third quarter savings hitting $10 million, the highest ever for a single quarter, I felt something strange. Apparently, John's impression was different. For some inexplicable reason our cost savings numbers were not showing up to Stanley's eight businesses, our primary customers. John had difficulty in putting our numbers in those business buckets or even on the corporate level. He could not see how Asia sourcing operations alone managed $26 million while the entire corporate productivity was about $90 million. I flew with my entire management team to New England and explained to him, the finance team and the business leaders the entire process of calculation. They all showed understanding, but linking it to the corporate performance record was the issue of paramount importance. It was a quagmire. John tersely said, "Deven, stop manufacturing numbers." It was the shock of my life. Among other things, I felt it was a signal that I had fallen from grace. I was fully aware that Stanley had not performed well in the third and the fourth quarters of 2002 and had missed the first quarter of 2003 and that this was taking a toll on John's health. Apart from my being his loyal entourage for twenty-one years, I had enjoyed his fatherly care, warmth and mentorship. He kept fostering my strengths. I had his great affection and now I was concerned for him.

John again invited me for lunch on January 2nd, 2003. Unlike previous lunches, I was not looking forward to this one. It was simply because I felt he became irrational, probably cracking under pressure. I guessed his demands would be unreasonable. Exactly as my hunch warned me, he gave me a report card on my 2002 performance, which was 'B minus'. He qualified this saying that my performance merited a B+ but he had expected me to do much better still, knowing me for more than twenty years. Then came the meat. He asked for two things: To close down the Taipei and Taichung operations in effective June 30th, 2003 and either move all staff China or dismiss them and then to transfer the entire Taiwan supplier base to China. My first reaction was to take him through the Taiwan and China phase-out and phase-in plan on which we had been working on and which he had blessed many times earlier. He did say it was absolutely important to execute the plan, but all of sudden he said, "Period."

He was grumpy. He did not allow me to say even a few words. I had never seen him in such a form. I had limited options; to tender my resignation on the spot, or to say, 'Okay I'll try my best.' Telling him the second option meant saying 'yes I will do it' when I knew my heart was saying that it was not possible to do it in six months simultaneously performing our regular tasks. He recognized my silence as a gesture to accept his demands, but I needed some time to make a proposal to him. He gave me four weeks to come back to him. The reason I did not tender my resignation right away was that Aditya's marriage was planned for March 9th, 2003. I wanted to be quiet until then. This experience was so horrible that I did not even touch my lunch. He noticed that and said my appetite seemed to have vanished. His concluding remark was that he expected me to execute it actually by March 31st but with my son's marriage scheduled during that month, a special consideration of moving it by three months had been made. However, I had already made up my mind right on the lunch table to quit Stanley in the first week of April.

On February 7th, I visited New England. I briefed John on our plan that was a gradual phase out from Taipei - ramping up our China team and closing the Taiwan offices by June 2004. He observed that the plan appeared to be realistic, and thanked me, but I felt I was not my usual self and he too business-like. Our meeting was brief and chilled. It was my sixth sense that he had made his decision to get rid of me. On April 4th, Claudia sent me an e-mail to call John immediately. What a coincidence, it was the week I had in mind for conveying my decision to quit. Apparently, John was ahead of me. He told me that he was eliminating my job effective April 11th, 2004 as part of the mass lay-off announcement of approximately 7% of Stanley's entire workforce. However, he gave me an option I could elect to leave earlier to spare myself from the ordeal of being laid off. I called him on the 8th. Thanking him for the opportunity, I told him that I learned about working in Taiwan and China, but now having obtained a new perspective on Japan looking from outside, its history, culture and behaviors of Japanese people compared with Taiwanese and Chinese people, I decided to quit immediately. He was apparently in the midst of chaos. I was appalled. To me he was always in command. It was shaking. I was sad. On the 11th, during my last week in office, I decided to send him a personal note as a friend of 21 years, not as his employee, with two observations. The first was that growth was not John's forte. He inherited Stanley on January 1st 1997 with its sales of US$2.5 billion and in 2002, six years later, sales were just $2.39 billion. In the intervening years revenue had hovered at around $2.5 billion, just flat. His track record during GE Audio and GE Medical was flawless. In the eighteen years of GE service he missed only two quarters. Secondly, I pointed out that he excelled in rationalization, creation of cost leadership, generating and freeing up cash, developing processes like product development and, above all, in execution of details. Finally I recommended to him as a loyal and concerned friend to move over. I thought I would be kicked for letting the emperor know that he had no clothes, however, to my surprise, John came back arguing logically that his track record of growth during the GE years was indeed phenomenal but admitting Stanley would not become another GE at least in the near future.

I sent out the following parting note to my Team.

Friends:

This is the 79th and the last edition of Inter-active Forum since its launch in July 2001.

ASO Team has come a long way in terms of professionalism, numbers driven/ values based, stretching to deliver commitments ... becoming the strategical arm of Stanley businesses during the last 22 months I've been here.

However, our task is not complete yet. In our ever-changing environment ... we've to anticipate change, adapt to the changes and enjoy the changes as we're going through this change. And continue this cycle over and over!

Therefore, we need to change again as I've decided to retire effective April 11th.

In my life, I had never thought that I'd ever come to Taiwan/ China to live and work. Mr. John Trani provided me with this exciting opportunity and I enjoyed every second of it. Every one of you accepted me and helped me grow. It was great as we learned in the moments of fun while building our executional capability ... brick by brick! And we're supported by Stanley businesses, global commodity teams, SAP & MCS partners.

Please extend to Mike Shin your continued superb support. His leadership will stretch ASO Team to Global Sourcing Team in boundaryless style ... from strength to strength!

I'm grateful for the knowledge, fun and friendship as we toiled and sweat ... together!

In the words of Bob Hope ... 'Thanks for precious memories!'

During the third week of May, I saw an announcement on Internet that John was to retire as CEO, The Stanley Works, effective December 31st, 2003. I called him to wish him the very best in his retirement. John was then a totally different person, relaxed, jovial and of course full of laughter.

Lesson

Never be afraid of speaking up your mind.

CHAPTER 25

THE DREAM CONTINUES...

The journey of a thousand miles starts with a single step...
Chinese Proverb

In July 2003 I started becoming restless to do something, which I wanted to do all my life but could not. I took inventory of my skills and assets. I was surprised by their richness. The first and foremost was many friends, so many friends who were eager to help in any discipline I wanted to venture. Second, of course, was my sourcing skill developed over a span of thirty-plus years. The third was the unique combination of my Indian heritage, long Japan residence and acculturation, and my China experience. There are tremendous opportunities and exciting times in the history to play a significant role among those three nations - culturally and commercially.

However, I wanted to ensure that my hunch had enough ground to bet my life on. Among my umpteen flights to Shanghai from Hong Kong, I once happen to sit next to a man who recommended seeing one individual, Benjamin (Ben) Zhai, at Egon Zehnder International, a global search company, based in Shanghai. Ben was one of the few individuals who looked into my eyes and said with this knowledge base it would be a sheer waste if I simply watch all the action that is going on between China and India from the sidelines. He did not let me leave his office until he got my commitment that I would indeed be initiating with my own venture. Ben, to me, turned to be 'Mr. Enabler'.

With the decision made, I looked around for some friends. During my Stanley days I was close to Jack Perkowski, Chairman and Chief Executive Officer, ASIMCO, based in Beijing. Theresa Dong, his executive assistant, a very warm hearted person, nailed Jack down to spend ten minutes out of his busy schedule, to guide me. Jack not only reaffirmed Ben's recommendation but also gave a list of four companies (three Indian and an American) who were exploring ways to get into China market to sell and/or buy. All the three Indian companies were publicly listed and had global network and influence. One company's executive director responded to my query within four hours. There was an instant click and we are now working on various possibilities. He is smart and knowledgeable with a global network. We became very good friends as well.

Formally, I launched my venture in February 2004. A friend in New Zealand suggested a company name, ICONASIA. Her rationale was that I am an Indian (I) working in China (hence 'C') and living in Japan (Nippon, 'N') and my domain would primarily be Asia. To my question of what the 'O' stood for, she has not responded to me yet but I believe it was my round face.

John Van Fleet, with whom I worked at GE YMS, is currently based in Shanghai and is acting as my window in Shanghai. He enjoys meeting people from all walks of life. To me he has his own 'mini United Nations' with global reach. For my needs he always has an answer. He connects me instantly with the right individuals.

Shanghai has become my home for two weeks every month. One of the secrets of my survival here is that Rajesh Prabhakar, the owner of the best Indian restaurant, Patiala Pearl, and his team of managers and chefs takes excellent care of me and my guests.

To me, visiting his restaurant is just like a homecoming. I do it almost everyday. Rajesh is our family friend.

My association with Sanyo Electric Co. Ltd. based in Osaka has been over thirty years. Emo Kamuro, 89, is credited with Sanyo's global growth for over fifty years but is very active even today. Mr. Kamuro and his esteemed colleague, Kiichiro Nakamura, 71, are two gentlemen who take exceptional care of me. Their affection towards me has no bounds. Norikazu Ito was our primary contact at Sanyo. Sanyo made GE Audio and Communication Products on an OEM basis, back in the 70's and 80's. Nori is now my partner in ICONASIA, Ltd.

While we have been planting seeds in many of our ventures, some of the efforts are in the harvesting mode. One amongst them is sourcing automotive components for a German automotive company specializing in high quality propeller shafts and double joints. The first shipment has been made in December 2004. Our first accomplishment is to become their excclusive purchasing agent for entire Asia (except India). My colleague, Geoffrey Wang, in Shanghai is driving it.

In the words of David Joseph Schwartz, all great achievements require time. Every institution goes through four phases:
- Gathering.
- Storming.
- Norming.
- Forming.

To a varying degree, we are still dabbling in the first three modes.

With our persistence and disciplined execution, we will endeavor to make ICONASIA a great enterprise to bridge Asia.

Lesson

You are NEVER late in life. It is not when you do but what you do that matters.

FINALE

God grant me the serenity to accept the things I cannot change, the courage to change the things I can, and the wisdom to know the difference...

Reinhold Niebuhr

Aarna Sakura, our grand daughter of nine months, Bitia (Vibha), Aditya, Renu and myself are healthy, happy and a fortunate global family. We count our blessings. Everyone shares our laughs ... but are a few to cry with us. My theory is to laugh - laugh heartily with full lungs.

We want to leave the following legacy when we depart from this beautiful earth.

"Renu and Deven was a couple who made a positive difference in the lives of people they came in contact with."

∎